REINCARNATION

A HOPE OF THE WORLD

Other Quest books by Irving Cooper:
The Secret of Happiness
Theosophy Simplified

Cover art by *Jane A. Evans*

REINCARNATION

A HOPE OF THE WORLD

IRVING S. COOPER

*This publication made possible with
the assistance of the Kern Foundation*
The Theosophical Publishing House
Wheaton, Ill. U.S.A.
Madras, India / London, England

Ninth printing. First Quest edition, 1979. Published by
The Theosophical Publishing House, a department of
The Theosophical Society in America.

Library of Congress Cataloging in Publication Data

Cooper, Irving Steiger, Bp., 1882 - 1935.
Reincarnation, a hope of the world.

  (A Quest book)
  Previously published under title: Reincarnation, the
hope of the world.
  1. Reincarnation. I. Title.
BP573.R5C6 1979   129'.4   79-11475
ISBN 0-8356-0528-0

Printed in the United States of America

CONTENTS

Preface

Introduction v

1 The Despair of the World 1

2 The Meaning of Reincarnation 11

3 The Purpose of Reincarnation 24

4 The Process of Reincarnation 35

5 The Proofs of Reincarnation: Objections
   and Arguments 48

6 The Proofs of Reincarnation: The Mem-
   ory of Past Lives 79

7 The Hope of the World 101

INTRODUCTION

In Palestine, on the slopes of Mount Hermon, about forty-five miles north of the Sea of Galilee, are scattered the ruins of an ancient city, Caesarea Philippi by name. One day, while approaching the outskirts of this city—if we may trust the story of the Gospels*—the Christian Master asked His disciples a question of such far-reaching importance that, had its full meaning been understood by later generations, the whole religious history of Western civilization would have been changed.

"Whom say the people that I am?" He asked.

To us the question is almost unintelligible, but the disciples apparently understood His meaning, for one answered that some people thought that Jesus was John the Baptist returned, for John had been beheaded some time before, while others of the disciples said that He was regarded as the reincarnation either of Elias or of Jeremias, both of whom had been dead for centuries. In short, the rumor was current that in the person of Jesus "one of the old prophets is risen again," which in-

* *Matt. XVI., 13-14. Mark VIII., 27-28. Luke IX., 18-19.*

dicates how wide-spread was the idea of reincarnation at the time.

It may be rightly objected, however, that Jesus Himself did not confirm any of the rumors; on the contrary, He apparently approved of the statement that He was the Son of God. While this is true it should be noticed that nowhere does He *deny* the truth of reincarnation. In fact, he affirms it in that well-known but little understood statement: But I say unto you, that Elias is come already, and they knew him not, but have done unto him whatsoever they listeth. . . Then the disciples understood that He spake unto them of John the Baptist.

Josephus implies, in his history of the wars of the Jews, that the idea of the rebirth of the soul was common among the people, and, judging from several striking passages in the Gospels in addition to those quoted, there is some evidence in support of this implication.

Reincarnation was also well-known to the Romans, for it is referred to by a number of the poets, while among the Greeks it was taught by several of the philosophers, chief among them Plato. Traces of the idea in a modified form are to be found in the ancient Egyptian religion, while in later Alexandria this teaching received much attention from the Neo-Platonists and Gnostics. It was sung in the Sagas of the Northmen and spread with the legends of the Gauls. It formed part of the mystic lore of the Druids, and even today a belief in the return of the soul still lingers among the Celtic peasantry of Ireland and of Brittany.

Strangely enough the idea of reincarnation was also current among the Indians on the American continents. From Alaska to Peru, among the Eskimos, the Sioux, the Zunis and the Incas particularly, the idea was taught by the priests and held by the tribesmen. Even among the natives of the Hawaiian Group, of Australia and of the Islands of the South Seas, the idea is not unknown.

It is in the Orient, however, that the teaching of reincarnation has spread most widely and exerted the greatest influence. It is the basic teaching of most of the religious and philosophical systems of India, and today throughout the Orient hundreds of millions of human beings accept the truth of reincarnation in about the same way that we accept the truth of gravity—as a great natural and inevitable law which it is foolish to question.

Obviously, then, reincarnation is one of the fundamental religious ideas of mankind, quite irrespective of its truth. Its universality is almost equal to the belief in the existence of a divine Power. The origin of the idea is unknown, for its roots strike so deep into the many layers of human thought deposited through the ages, that it is impossible to trace them to their beginnings. It is surmised that the belief in reincarnation antedates all known history, and certainly traces of it are to be found in all religious and in the myths of nearly all primitive peoples.

Unfortunately, as the idea of reincarnation has come to us from the past, it is nearly always associated with misconceptions and superstitions. No doubt this is due to its very antiquity, but, whatever may be the cause, the superstitions are so repellent to Western ways of thinking, and the misconceptions so illogical, that great discredit has been cast on the philosophical value of the central idea itself. Who is it that yearns to be born as a dog or a blue-bottle fly?

Yet back of all the fancies clustering round the belief in the rebirth of the soul there must surely be a vital truth, else the idea of reincarnation could not have endured for so many thousands of years, nor could it have attracted so many able thinkers.

Part of the work of the Theosophical Society has been to present the vital truth of reincarnation free from misconceptions and superstitions, and it is astounding how quickly thoughtful people have come to regard it with favor. Forty years ago only a few score of people had even taken reincarnation seriously, much less made it their working philosophy of life; now it is probable that millions of people in the Western world look upon reincarnation as the most logical explanation of many social, religious, and philosophical problems. The acceptance of reincarnation has spread far beyond the limits of the Theosophical Society.

This is due not to any desire to return to earth— for most people at first shrink from this—but to the inherent reasonableness of reincarnation and to its extraordinary value in explaining the most baffling of human problems. Those in touch with the currents of modern thought are convinced that reincarnation will soon be generally accepted by most thinking people not because of any passing popularity, but because of its sheer power to convince, to illuminate, and to inspire. It is surely destined to be the Great Idea of this century, even as the idea of evolution transformed the conceptions of the last.

CHAPTER 1

THE DESPAIR OF THE WORLD

The restlessness of our time is due largely to unanswered questions. While it is true that the frontier separating the known from the unknown has been pressed back some little way, yet we are beginning to see that the size of the conquered territory is smaller than we thought. To the casual reader science is practically omniscient, but the trained observer is fully aware that he is surrounded by enigmas. To the devout churchman modern Christianity is an impregnable fortress, but the wiser eyes of many of its leaders are watching anxiously the ominous cracks appearing in its walls under the terrific fire of advancing criticism.

A century or so ago when, as the outcome of the grapple between science and theology, unreasoning faith in tradition and dogma began to give way to research and reason, a furious questioning of life and of the world arose. Nothing was exempt. The current ideas of God and the soul, of revelation and destiny, were torn to fragments as thoroughly as every speculative conception of the phenomenal world. It was a period of intellectual revolution, and the thinkers of the race, exulting in their freedom, determined to destroy utterly every falsehood which had weighed them down. Unfortunately, in the hurry of destruction, they cast aside many a truth.

Materialism was the inevitable outcome of such a reaction, and at first it did seem able to answer satisfactorily the questions propounded. Men hopefully persuaded themselves that all things and all events in the universe, including the workings of the mind, could easily and logically be explained in terms of matter. It was believed that there was nothing in the universe but force and matter and the laws governing them. It was joyfully affirmed that the old beliefs, which had kept civilization so long in confinement, were dead forever. God was a myth, the soul a fancy, destiny the grinding of the world-machine, religion a tissue of childish legends interwoven with more or less wholesome ethics. And so, on the morning of this new intellectual day, rationalistic science overthrew its ancient antagonist, theology, and strode on to further conquests.

It was a period of resistless enthusiasm. A feverish thirst for exploration drove men on from discovery to discovery. It was felt that soon the last of Nature's secrets would be known. Experiments in physics showed that Nature was synonymous with law; the curiosity of the chemist laid open the hidden structure of matter; the Darwinian theory of evolution revealed order and purpose in the complex realm of living things. In the crust of the layered earth was read the marvelous story of ages long since past; great telescopes gathered up the light-waves from giant nebulae and from millions of distant suns and cast them upon the photographic plate; the study and dissection of the human body gave rise to many sciences—anatomy, physiology, histology, embryology, psychology, medicine, and the like. The mastery of the world seemed near, and mankind was thrilled—with the omniscience of youth.

We have grown a little older since then, and though there is still enthusiasm, it is somewhat tempered by maturity. The first rough-and-hasty methods of research are slowly being replaced by more refined and skillful procedure. We are now engaged in going over the waste-heaps of ideas cast off during the last four centuries, taking the same minute care that is being bestowed upon tailings once discarded as valueless by the refiners of precious ore, and in the midst of the rubbish much of value is being found.

It is becoming evident also that some of our most prized treasures are only fool's gold, glittering but worthless. Science has had to throw away theory after theory, religion dogma after dogma, philosophy speculation after speculation. Consequently, there is not a little uneasiness and anxious turning one to another asking what will be the outcome of it all. It has become evident that many of the old theories and dogmas are untenable, but what can be found to replace them? The search for knowledge has resolved itself into a complex series of questions, which, remaining unanswered, has bred uncertainty, and out of uncertainty restlessness has sprung. Materialism has been discarded, truly, but the religious thought of the new age is still groping its way to adequate expression.

Does God exist and is there a moral law at the heart of the universe? If so, why then is death everywhere, the weak overcome by the strong, the lesser preyed upon by the greater?

"How lizard fed on ant, and snake on him,
 And kite on both; and how the fish-hawk robbed
 The fish-tiger of that which it had seized;
 The shrike chasing the bulbul, which did hunt
 The jewelled butterflies; till everywhere
 Each slew a slayer and in turn was slain,
 Life living upon death. So the fair show
 Veiled one vast, savage, grim conspiracy
 Of mutual murder, from the worm to man,
 Who himself kills his fellow . . ."

If God exists why is there so much misery in the world, so much undeserved suffering, so many unearned gifts and opportunities? Why are strong men suddenly struck blind, innocent children scourged with disease, nursing mothers killed by some drunken fool speeding in a motor car? Must we agree with Mill that if there is a God either He does not care or else He is so powerless that He cannot change conditions? To speak of an inscrutable Providence does not solve our problem; it only affirms our ignorance.

In this world is right rewarded and wrong punished? Observation tells us that it is not. Many times the criminal goes free, the innocent is imprisoned. To mediocrity come rank and wealth, to real worth hardship and despair. Envy and malice hound ability to the grave; the hands of the populace applaud the successful trickster. The Churches which yearn to help mankind are slowly losing ground; the strongholds of vice are apparently becoming ever more strongly entrenched. Goodness in business is a handicap, we are told, for in the marketplace the saint is a failure and the gambler supreme. The Christlike virtues are helpless in the grasp of might, and against our wills we must arm ourselves to protect our homes from ravage.

A little while ago a man was released from a prison after spending nearly a third of his life within its walls. He had been convicted on circumstantial evidence and, though protesting his innocence, was sentenced for life. Twenty years later the real criminal confessed to the crime on his death-bed, and the innocent man was released, a wreck physically, morally, and mentally, for such is the disgrace of our penal system. A minister of the Gospel, a man of deep feeling and wide sympathies, whose work brought him frequently into touch with released prisoners, met this man and tried to console him and to bring him back into touch with Christianity. He felt the weakness of words, so he simply put his hand on the shoulder of the man and told him to try to be patient and strong, to trust the loving Will of God and the Promise of Christ. The effect upon the prisoner was significant. He straightened up, his eyes blazing with the concentrated bitterness of twenty years of undeserved suffering, and in a voice hoarse from the deadly fluff of the jute-mill, asked these searching questions:

"Do you mean to tell me that it was God's will that sent me to prison? If He is just and loving why didn't He save me from such a fate? What had I done to deserve such suffering? I was an honest man and I loved and worked for my family. And then they sent me to that hell for a crime I didn't commit. Was it God's will that left my wife and two children to starve? Where are they now? I haven't heard from them for years. They may be starving or dead or—worse. And look at me, a wreck—offal flung on the dung-heap of civilization. And then you tell me that it was all the will of God! Get out! I want none of your God!"

And the minister went away a sorrowing man, for he had no way and no arguments whereby he could convince the released prisoner that God exists, and that He is good.

Religion tells us of a world to come, and would have us understand that there our wrongs will be recompensed, our sins forgiven, our ignorance dispelled. Through all the centuries men's eyes have turned longingly to that world, and they have endured the trials of this for what has been promised hereafter. But if God created a world, apparently so wretchedly arranged as this, what hope have we, in the name of logic, to expect anything better in heaven? If there is little justice here, why more there?

If all souls are equal at birth why are human destinies so terribly unequal? Are we to fall back upon the hopeless doctrine of predestination and the elect? Why is not every soul given a chance to develop its powers? Is it all a matter of chance? Can we conceive of a divinely-ordered universe in which such matters as human lives are left to the blind working of chance? Is it not significant that all other events in the physical universe are guided by natural law?

So far as this world is concerned, human equality is a myth, despite the orations of vote-seeking politicians. We are unequal physically, mentally, morally, and spiritually, while opportunity and limitation seem always to be playing a game of tag with our plans.

Some men have strong and healthy bodies; others are frail and diseased. Some have grace and physical refinement; others are gross and coarsely grained. Some have quick and capacious brains; others are dull and limited in thought. Think, too, how completely our standing in the world is affected by what we are physically. Equality?

Equality is denied by every fact in Nature!

In one of our large cities, for many years there was to be seen a little cripple seated at the street corner on a piece of carpet. He was certainly over forty years of age, but had a body the size of a boy of ten, and his arms and legs were so twisted and distorted that it was unpleasant even to look at him. For years he had kept himself alive by selling pencils and papers, and the limits of his intellectual universe were bounded by the street-crossing at which he sat. Contrast the limitations of his life— the physical suffering, the dim yearning for friendship, the colorless days, the narrow horizons—with the many opportunities and friends which have come to us. If we believe there is a divine Power, then that Power is responsible for this man's destiny, either directly by placing a soul without stain in this crippled body, or indirectly by creating a world in which such tragedies can take place.

Why are there so many terrible inequalities in environment? One child is born in an Eskimo hut, doomed by its very birth to a life of the utmost narrowness. Another is born in the midst of an advanced civilization, with every educational and cultural advantage. One is born in the dark, foul room of a crowded tenement, reared in rags and taught in the gutter. Another is born in a home of refinement, reared in the best of surroundings and taught in an excellent school. One grows up to be a shambling beggar of alms, the other a leader of men and an honor to the State.

If there *are* souls and they are equal at birth why should there be this favoritism? Why is one wailing infant condemned by the very conditions of its birth to a life of misery and deprivation, and another to good fortune and endless opportunities? Is God's love, mercy, or justice made manifest in this? Is there no law or purpose in the assignment of our respective destinies?

Why are there so many inequalities in opportunities? One man may work hard all his life and in the end, through some accident, become a charity patient in a dreary hospital or the inmate of a home. Another inherits a vast estate and possibly a title, has a yacht and several motor cars, travels widely and draws largely upon the luxuries of the world. He is an idler, a parasite, a useless member of society, but his hands are filled with treasure. Why should this be so, if not a sparrow falleth unknown? It is not correct to answer that it is all a matter of work and of intellect, for many bright men of industry have failed, and many fools have money constantly springing up under their fingertips.

Turn where we will, the world is full of inequalities, of startling contrasts, which are inexplicable in the light of current religious teaching. We feel instinctively that there *must* be Divinity at the back of all things and all events, but we are unable to *prove* it by pointing to the conditions of the world. On the contrary, moral chaos seems more in evidence than moral order. It is any wonder that the ranks of the churchless are increasing year by year?

It is true that Christianity has endeavored to solve these problems, usually along two lines— original sin and the will of God—but neither answer satisfies the modern mind. The first answer fails because we have become convinced that Adam never existed, and that therefore there could have been no original sin. The second answer fails because it makes God directly responsible for all the suffering in the world, especially that which arises from birth conditions, and we rather shrink from worshiping such a Being as that!

These problems of religion are the despair of the modern world. They seem impossible of answer, and yet unanswered they make ineffective the teachings of religion, and materialize the hopes of men. A master-key is needed to solve them, to make real again the life of the spirit, to make strong the faltering trust in the goodness of God and the purpose of life. In reincarnation that master-key is found.

CHAPTER 2

THE MEANING OF REINCARNATION

Few people ever take the trouble to think out just what views they hold about the world. If they did they would be much surprised to find out how much is taken for granted as being true without any real thought about the matter at all.

When a child is born, for example, we take for granted that its consciousness was created with its body. The basis for this assumption, of course, is easy to be seen. In the child we see apparently the development of the consciousness with the growth of the body, and in old age the disappearance of the consciousness with the death of the body. From these parallel changes we receive the impression that the brain *produces* the consciousness, but this is not by any means the only explanation of the facts.

With the facts exactly as they are, it is quite possible that the brain is not the originator, but only the instrument of consciousness, and that the mind—using the term in its broadest sense—is quite distinct from the brain. According to the delicacy and response of the instrument will be the physical expression of the consciousness using it.

The brain of an infant has little power of response because it is too plastic and unorganized, and so the mind using it can impress but little of itself upon it. As the child grows and the brain becomes more organized, the mind of the child is much more in evidence, not so much because of the growth of consciousness itself, but because of the improvement in the instrument transmitting the consciousness. In old age the brain becomes less responsive, and hence the physical expression of the mind is dimmed. At death the instrument is destroyed and therefore the consciousness can no longer make itself manifest physically, at least in any normal way, but this does not imply in the slightest the annihilation of the mind. Putting it tersely, the consciousness of man is no more dependent upon the brain for *existence* than is a musician upon his violin, but both instruments are necessary for *expression* in the physical world.

This is the viewpoint from which to approach the study of reincarnation. The mind is not the brain. The brain is a delicately-arranged receiving and transmitting instrument composed of millions of nerve-cells with their branches and binding tissue; the waking consciousness is that small part of the total consciousness of man to which the brain responds. As conscious human beings we can and do exist just as well without a physical body as with it, both after death and *before birth*.

The human consciousness exists before birth and even before conception—this is the first fundamental fact of reincarnation. The infant is young in body only, for using that body and seeking ever more and more to manifest itself through the agency of the brain and nervous system is a mature consciousness which has had much human experience in the past during other lives on earth.

The second great fact of reincarnation is that the soul or conscious self of man is a growing thing, and that its development from its first awakening to the gaining of its splendid maturity, is extended over an enormous period of time, measured in tens of thousands of years. The soul is "perfect" at the beginning of its human experience only in the same sense that a seed is perfect, for there is just as much difference relatively between a "young" and "old" soul as there is between an acorn and an oak. It is permissible to speak of this growth of the soul as an evolution of consciousness, but we ought to be careful in our thinking not to confuse such growth with the evolution of physical bodies, which is the subject-matter of the Darwinian and other evolutionary theories.

Such physical evolution is carried on by means of birth, cell-growth, parenthood, death, new bodies ever being produced by the old, thus giving rise to a continuity of physical forms. The whole tendency of physical evolution is from simple to complex, at one end of the organic series being the single cell without organs or structures, and at the other the extraordinarily complex body of man with its millions of cells grouped into organs and tissues.

The evolution of consciousness takes place by a process of ensoulment of the evolving physical forms. This process of repeated embodiment is known as reincarnation. It is a universal process, and prevails not only in the human kingdom but throughout the whole of Nature. Whenever we find a living form, the consciousness of that form is also evolving, using temporarily for that purpose the physical form in order that it may gain physical experience. Reincarnation is the means by which hosts of evolving lives, of all degrees of development, are brought into association with evolving physical forms of all degrees of complexity.

For the gaining of experience, it is obvious that the evolution of the consciousness must match the evolution of the form, and through the automatic processes of Nature this is always the case. Thus by means of the instrumentality of the human body is made manifest a highly-developed type of consciousness not found in the lower kingdoms, because the human body with its marvelous brain structure is far more adapted to the needs of such a consciousness than is the relatively undeveloped brain of, say, such an animal as a mule.

Is it not evident from a study of Nature that in the great plan of things little attention is paid to the preservation of forms? Death is universal; everywhere physical bodies are being sacrificed to keep other physical bodies alive. Mineral forms are broken up to furnish food for plants; plants are sacrificed to animals; animals to man. From the physical point of view Nature is a house of death, and this very fact has been not only the despair of philosophy, but the chief argument of science against the religious belief in God.

In the light of reincarnation it is recognized that the reason Nature cares so little for physical bodies is that they are really of minor importance. Their one function is to serve the growing consciousness as a means for gaining experience. Consciousness, with its power of memory, is the important thing, and consciousness is carefully preserved. Nature destroys forms lavishly because the consciousness using those forms cannot die, and as all memories and faculties are retained by the consciousness after the death of the physical bodies, nothing of value is, in reality, lost.

We may define reincarnation, then, by saying that it is a plan whereby imperishable conscious beings are supplied with physical bodies appropriate to their stage of growth, and through which they can come in contact with the lessons of physical life.

From the standpoint of reincarnation the earth—and quite likely the whole universe—is a great school. It was brought into existence for educational purposes, and the whole plan of evolution is designed to give just the amount and kind of experience which is needed to stimulate the growth of an almost infinite series of living things, of which the known physical kingdoms form only a small part.

Just as a child goes to school day after day, learning lessons, gathering experience and passing from grade to grade, so do we in our greater soul-life come here to earth many times, learning lessons, gathering experience, and passing from one social grade to another.

We commenced our human evolution as savages, because our moral and intellectual powers had hardly begun to stir. After a few lives amid such primitive conditions, we developed some slight trace of mental faculty and moral response, and were then born into some rude type of civilization. Much suffering marked our various incarnations because we were willful, passionate, and sometimes cruel; but as the centuries advanced and we reaped many an evil harvest grown from evil seed of our own sowing, the voice of conscience—which is only the summarized memory of past experience—became more insistent and we began to refrain slightly from wrong-doing. As incarnation followed incarnation in rather rapid succession, we grew intellectually and morally through contact with the people about us, through the discipline of the law, and through the very pressure of physical existence. We were still ignorant folk, able to perform only unskilled labor, but nevertheless life on earth taught us slowly how to become something better, as it does every other human being. Life after life passed, each with its joys and sorrows, its opportunities and its difficulties, its successes and its failures, until we became skilled artisans. Here we learned of a higher standard of living, and slowly began to think, instead of constantly being swayed by unreasoning feelings and prejudices. Gradually, as the lives on earth followed one another, for human evolution is painfully slow, we spent a longer time between incarnations away from earth in the different conditions of the unseen world. As a result our mental faculties unfolded more rapidly, our moral perceptions increased, our spirituality began to awaken. Many of us are a little past this level of evolution now, and because of the enormous amount of experience we have gained during other lives on earth we are developing into thinkers and occupy a relatively important position in the social scale. Some of our fellow-pupils are more advanced than we and are acknowledged by the world as the leaders of civilization, either by the splendor of their intellectual powers, the ability they display as statesmen, the beauty of their moral character, or the kindness of their spiritual insight.

In this there is no favoritism; it is only a matter of growth. The level they have reached we ourselves shall some day attain, if we only take advantage of our opportunities. They are more advanced and have greater power, because their evolutionary development started at an earlier period than did ours. We do not cry "favoritism" because in a school some pupils are in the upper classes while others are in the lower. It is all a matter of time, for after a while the pupils in the lower classes will themselves be in the higher. The same plan is followed in the World-School; ahead of us are "older" souls, behind us "younger" souls, the procession is endless, for while millions pass through the various classes one by one and eventually graduate, there are always other millions treading in their footsteps. In this there is no injustice but only a definite educational scheme.

So, in the light of reincarnation, we may picture humanity as marching up a giant stairway, the lower part of which can be seen emerging from the twilight of the beginning of things, the upper part vanishing into the glory of Divinity. How long the stairway is we do not know, but this is really not important. The important thing to realize is that we are standing now upon one of the steps and that the position we hold in the procession marks definitely our stage in growth. Such a realization ought to be an inspiration to us, for then we know that the great men and women of the world tell us in their persons and achievements what we with effort may become.

We are always the same individualities, although we may, during any one incarnation, take birth in a masculine body, and in another in a feminine body. This is necessary in order to balance and round out our development. Is it not noticeable that in the Christlike characters of history there is a singular and exquisite blending of the masculine and feminine virtues?

In each incarnation we have a different physical body, a different name, and may have different souls acting as parents, but these changes do not in the slightest imperil our individuality. Our minds are not drawn at birth, as some philosophers think, from a great ocean of consciousness, nor at death do we lose the sense of personal existence. If this were really the case reincarnation would be meaningless, and evolution the cruel sport of some transcendent Being.

As souls we are sexless, but our physical bodies are given sex by the plan of evolution, in order that there might be social groups, homes, family responsibilities, dependent children, sacrifices of personal pleasure, joys of affectionate relationships, contacts of different temperaments, for all these have enormous educational value.

We have been given physical bodies needing food, clothing, shelter, because through the efforts put forth to secure these things for ourselves and for others, the whole complex fabric of civilization has been woven, and the physical, moral, and mental powers of humanity have been stimulated to activity. Notice how often in a tropical climate, where everything is supplied by Nature to meet the wants of man, the people are backward, lazy, and relatively uncivilized. When outer circumstances are such that we are forced to think and forced to work in order to live and succeed, our growth is the most rapid. We are most favored when life is most difficult.

To a great extent we have been left to solve our own social, political, and religious problems, and some people have advanced this as an argument to prove that there is no overwatching spiritual Power. But surely modern educational methods have demonstrated that the best way to awaken initiative, intellectual power, and ability to act with skill, is to give the children who are being taught a chance to *exercise* their faculties. To tell them everything and explain everything may develop the memory and the power of imitation, but it leaves the child hopelessly weak in other ways. What is true of children is also true of the pupils in the World-School, and if we only used enough common sense to apply the principles of sound pedagogy to the circumstances of daily life, we should find an adequate and helpful explanation of why we are left to learn through our mistakes. We have indeed been helped by the spiritual Teachers of the world far more often than we realize—were not the great religions of the world founded by Them?—but nevertheless, it is true that as a general rule mankind has been left to find its pathway alone. In no other way probably could the lessons of the world have been so thoroughly learned by mankind, and civilization brought to the point where it is realized that, in order to endure, society must be built upon a solid foundation of Brotherhood.

Reincarnation does not mean that the human soul can be reborn in an animal body. This belief is to be found in the myths of primitive peoples, in popular Hinduism and Buddhism, and even in the writings of Plato, but it is obviously a superstition and not a fact. To think of a human being, endowed with keen sensibilities, moral perception, and intellectual power, as being reborn after death in the body of an unmoral and unintelligent animal, is certainly the abyss of illogic and could serve no moral or evolutionary process whatsoever in the universe. Every process of Nature has always been found to have a definite purpose, and reincarnation is no exception to the rule.

Nor does reincarnation necessarily imply that we are reborn immediately after death, although in rare cases this may happen. A series of investigations into the past lives of some two hundred and fifty people, which was laboriously carried out a few years ago, showed that while the period between death and the next succeeding birth may, in the case of an undeveloped savage, be exceedingly short, yet a highly-evolved human being may remain away from earth for several centuries. The average period between incarnations for an intelligent man or woman is in the neighborhood of five hundred years, although the variations in this interval are so great, because of a multitude of causes, that it is impossible to state an average universally applicable.

Many people, when their attention is first drawn to reincarnation, dislike the idea immensely. They have not the slightest desire to be reborn, and so, without the least attempt to consider the matter, dismiss the idea as foolish. Mere dislike, however, disproves nothing. Indeed, most new truths are disliked. Do we not recall the storm of ridicule and the vigor of anathema which greeted the idea of evolution? There is no opposition so intense as that which is aroused by new ideas. A hasty rejection of reincarnation, therefore, may be thoroughly human, but it does not disprove its truth. The idea of reincarnation improves upon acquaintance, for usually our dislike is due, not to the central idea itself, but to some misconception concerning it which we have assumed to be true.

Our opposition to reincarnation arises largely because existence on earth is not easy. We are not really opposed to reincarnation merely as a process of return to earth, although we think we are, but to the associated thought that if we are reborn we must go through the trials of earth-life again. Our natural shrinking from this is the real cause of our opposition to reincarnation. We seldom look at life from the standpoint of its opportunities for growth, but nearly always measure it according to its power to cater to our desire for pleasure, idleness, position, honors, amusements. Because we are oftentimes denied these coveted things, which are of no educational value, and given instead hardships, labor, sorrows, failures, problems which teach us most quickly, we are violently opposed to any repetition of the process. How swiftly our opposition to reincarnation would fade away if we were guaranteed, upon our return to earth, the granting of all our desires!

If we will only remember, however, that the very experiences which are most difficult to bear teach us the greatest lessons of life, and that every pain we suffer, every hardship we endure, every failure which carries us downwards to defeat, means in the end more power to achieve, we shall look upon reincarnation with different eyes. If we think only of personal pleasure, reincarnation may be as uncomfortable to contemplate as a number of years of hard study in a school, but if we think of our usefulness to the world and the happiness we can give to others, then the thought of reincarnation fills us with enthusiasm and the will to attain. Further it should not be forgotten that much of the pain and suffering of human existence are due to our disregard of certain moral principles, and that when we learn to cooperate with the Law of Action and Reaction the result will always bring happiness, whereas disregard of it entails suffering and misery.

CHAPTER 3

THE PURPOSE OF REINCARNATION

The chief purpose of reincarnation is education. To this end we are born again and again on earth, not because of any external pressure, but because we, as *souls*, desire to grow. The driving-power at the back of reincarnation, which brings us to earth again, is the thirst for experience, the desire for knowledge, the yearning to mingle in the throb and rush of physical existence. To many people, whose lives here have been rather difficult, these desires seem inconceivable. The reason is that satiety kills out desire; a man who has just eaten a hearty dinner has no desire to think of other meals. In the same way, at the end of an incarnation, it is to be expected that we should have little desire for re-birth. Furthermore, our waking consciousness is only a portion of our actual consciousness, and our deeper selves often realize the need of that for which our outer selves do not care. This is the case with reincarnation; the physical consciousness, limited in outlook to the narrow horizons of a single earth-life, does not desire to be reborn, but the soul consciousness, having a splendid goal in view, is anxious to return.

In the vague ideas which are current regarding the human soul, it is not realized that power, wisdom, and character are all the results of an age-long education, and not the carelessly-scattered gifts of some whimsical destiny. There is soul growth as well as physical growth; there is an awakening of mental faculty during a whole series of lives in much the same way as there is an awakening of the mind at the beginning of each life on earth during that period we call childhood.

Life's great purpose is to develop our inherent powers. As we grow we do not *add* anything unto ourselves; we only arouse that which we have already slumbering within. Exactly the same process takes place when a seed sprouts; the germ within merely begins to unfold what is already contained within it. Growth is the stirring of latent powers and faculties to active expression. We, as souls, contain within ourselves everything we shall have hereafter, and the purpose of a series of lives on earth is to bring to us those experiences which will most rapidly awaken all our latent faculties and bring them into action.

Within each soul infinity lies hidden; in a sense each human being is the center of the universe, for God lives equally in all. If the character of our neighbor is adorned with a virtue which we have nòt, if he is equipped with a sterling quality which we admire, it is not that he has been given more than we, but that he has awakened into activity that particular virtue or quality sooner than we. If we wish to become like him, there is nothing to prevent our making the efforts which surely will bring our desire to fruition.

The glorious imagery of the gifted artist, the divine harmonies of the inspired musician, the keen mentality and patience of the scientist, the profundity of the philosopher, the wisdom of the born teacher—all these powers, and many more, lie hidden within us awaiting the time when we shall arouse them with the magic of the will.

There is neither great nor small, old nor young, wise nor ignorant, from the Godward side of the universe; all is God. But from the formward side God is expressed in different degrees of power, according to the capacity of the form. If the form be dense and unresponsive, as is the body of a savage, but little of the indwelling Divinity can manifest itself; if the form be pure, refined, and far-evolved, the inward God is able to shine forth with such blinding glory that we bow our heads in reverence and adoration. This is what St. Paul meant by the Christ within.

The evolution of forms is one of the functions of the World-School, but this is only one side of the whole process, for by growth we imply not only the development of forms in this and other worlds, but also the unfolding of the powers of consciousness. As growth takes place, the immeasurable Life behind is able ever more and more to manifest its beauty and its power. On the matter side of evolution is seen the slow transformation of mineral to plant, plant to animal, animal to man, man to superman; on the life side is seen the overbrooding spiritual Life gradually learning to inhabit and control these bodies built of matter.

We are a race of resplendent spiritual Beings—such has ever been the message of the Seers of all ages—who descended from our high estate at some period hidden in the mists of the illimitable past, in order to gain the mastery of matter such as is taught in a material solar system. At the time we commenced our evolution in the universe of matter, we found it impossible to interpret the meaning of its vibrations or to make the matter respond to the changes of our consciousness. Thus, while we possessed all the powers of our divine Father, they were as yet merely potential, latent, so far as outer existence was concerned. As aeon after aeon swept on in unhurried flight we began slowly to force matter to obey our will, until now, as human beings, we have progressed to the stage where we can understand physical vibrations—the slowest of all —and control a physical body; where we are able, partially at least, to understand the meaning of the vibrations of the astral world and assume some control over our emotional body; but where we know little as yet of those regions in which dwell mind and soul.

It is helpful to the young student to bear in mind that the physical body of a human being is surrounded and interpenetrated by a luminous ovoid composed of the emotional, mental, and soul bodies, in much the same way that the unseen mental and astral worlds surround and interpenetrate the earth. The analogy, however, should not be carried farther. All these bodies are but forms in which the Spirit is unfolding; even the soul body itself may be thought of as a radiant and flashing chalice of subtle matter in which is glowing a fragment of the Life that is God. But the Spirit in man, the life of the soul body, does not evolve, but rather is the infinite source of those qualities which, one by one, are expressed in the living garments of the soul we speak of as bodies.

Thus we have, in this World-School, old and young physical bodies whose age is measured by the years which stretch between the cradle and the grave; also we have old and young souls whose vaster span of life is measured by hundreds of incarnations on earth; the Spirit alone is without measure, without age, without limit—the Source of all things.

What greater stimulus to courage and valiant exertion than the knowledge that the loftiest ideal of which we dream, the mightiest powers for which we long, the superb beauty of character to which we aspire, are all to be found within ourselves! To win them petitions need not be offered, and prayers are useless; we must *work* for their development, even as we labor hours at the piano to gain the power of musical expression. We stand like men above a buried treasure, and all we have to do is dig.

Every particle of wisdom stored up by the soul increases the precious treasure which we come here to gain, even as every drop of attar of roses falling from the still adds richness to the fragrant perfume which has already been gathered. But soul-wisdom can be gained in no other way than by plucking in the gardens of the world the sweet and bitter blossoms of love and hate, action and sloth, success and failure, joy and sorrow, peace and turmoil. We grow as gradually we learn to master these conflicting forces and move with steady feet in the midst of a storm, or to take full advantage of a time of calm.

When we are reborn Nature is concerned primarily with only one thing, and that is our education. She does not try to amuse us or give us a good time; she teaches us through experience. Everything has its teaching value and broadening effect, and we should feel honored when life is hardest, for then it is that special pains are being taken with our education. What to us is usually regarded as a hardship or a sorrow is usually training of the greatest value. Our mistake lies in not looking at life from the standpoint of education; if we did, many of the most puzzling problems would disappear.

We should not, however, confuse Nature's plan of education with that of the human teacher. There are two kinds of education: the education of the memory, which crowds the mind with facts more or less logically arranged according to the capacity of the student; and the education of the faculties, which sounds the depths of the inner nature and calls forth to activity the powers that are hidden there. The first is the usual method of the pedagogue, the second that used in the World-School.

We are beginning to realize that real education is not limited to instruction in the various branches of learning—languages, mathematics, science, philosophy—which at best but stimulate the intellectual faculties; education in its truest sense should round out the whole character by building up a noble morality, encouraging generous emotions, disciplining the mind into accurate ways of thinking, teaching skill in action, awakening the power of the will, and developing the capacity to realize the Divine Presence.

No educational institution built by man ever attempted such instruction in full; the world is the only school which offers the entire curriculum. It might be even truer to say that the world is a great university, exquisitely adapted, down to its smallest detail, to the education of the swarming millions of living creatures which dwell upon its surface, in its interior, and within the atmosphere surrounding it. Each experience which comes to us, great or small, is part of the teaching. Naturally, we do not all attend the same classes or study the same lessons, for we are not all of the same soul-age, but every living thing—atom, microbe, plant, bird, animal, man, superman, or angel—receives just those experiences which are needed to insure its next step forward in evolution.

Unfortunately, we are far from being convinced of this. It may be true, we admit, for other people, but not for ourselves. We are constantly picturing to ourselves different surroundings in which we are sure we could grow more rapidly, and as constantly we ignore the very lessons which our present circumstances in life are endeavoring to teach us.

For some reason few of us take advantage of the teaching of daily life, unless forced to do so by some bitter experience. It often takes many lives to learn a single lesson of right and wrong, which might easily have been grasped in a year if we had applied ourselves to the problem, instead of thinking, as is usually our habit, that we have been injured or unhappily treated, and abusing Fate for her malignity. We run hither and thither like children after bright butterflies, and generally our mercurial attention receives but vague impressions from the valuable lessons which are offered. And so these same lessons are patiently repeated day after day, year after year, life after life, until finally their meaning dawns upon our inner vision. Sometimes the lessons which we persist in ignoring must be taught by pain in order to hold our wandering attention; sometimes they come with pleasures and captivating things which arouse desire. The loving Mother is always sublimely patient and uses many ways to teach her children.

If we were apt pupils our lives would be much freer from suffering than they are. Pain comes to

us because of our ignorance, our willful disobedi-
ence, and our inattention. If we were eager to learn,
if we joyfully welcomed each event as a gift for our
helping, if we cooperated with the Godward sweep
of evolution instead of stubbornly resisting it, our
growth would be rapid and our happiness unmarred.
How long will it take us to realize that Divine Love
is the matrix in which the universe is embedded,
and that Divine Wisdom guides the vibration of
every atom as well as the swing of the planets,
the life of the least of us as well as the destinies of
nations?

The memory of the experiences through which
we have gone, and the recognition of their relationships to one another, constitute knowledge.
Wisdom, however, is the realization of the inner
meaning and spiritual purpose of the oft-repeated
events of life. Thus wisdom is the essence distilled
from knowledge by the alchemy of the soul.

If we look deep into our own natures and un-
flinchingly study each hidden thought and motive,
we shall find that the cause of much of our sorrow
is selfishness, the longing to possess things and
persons for ourselves, our very own. Fundamentally
selfishness is a unifying tendency; it seeks to col-
lect and gather in, and to make each individual
"I" the center of the universe. Selfishness is a distorted and warped reflection in matter of the all-
embracing unity of the Spirit. On the spiritual
plane we know, as spiritual Intelligences, that we
are one with all living beings, but when that pure

insight is darkened and veiled by the bodies we wear, the sense of unity becomes limited to our own little circles, to our own wants and desires, and so is changed to selfishness.

As the wheel of life and death turns on its unswerving way, we learn by bitter lessons to extend the limits of our individual circles so as to draw within them wife and children. For them we labor, because dimly we realize that they are in some way one with us, and we become selfish for the family. As the days of schooling continue, we begin to look upon certain friends as part of ourselves and learn to serve them with the same assiduity as heretofore we served our families. Much later still, this group-selfishness expands to include the whole nation, and finally the entire world; our selfishness has been transmuted to spirituality, for we look upon every being as ourselves and exclude none from our circles. This is the level at which stands the Saviors of the world.

Though we have not as yet reached this marvelous level of spirituality, nevertheless we, as souls, are old, very old, and in a deep hidden layer of our consciousness reside wonderful and romantic memories of an age-long past spent in other lands and in other bodies. We have loved many times before with blinding passion; in stormy incarnations we have hated and fought and killed, with anger in our hearts. Grief has torn us again and again at the death of the bodies of those who were dear to us, and yet again and again we have met and lived and worked with those same dear ones when they and we have taken new bodies.

How utterly absurd to regard as heathen all the people who do not worship God in the same fashion, with the same ceremonies and under the same name as we, for in other lives and lands we have loved and reverenced the very manifestations of the Divine which now we refuse to recognize. How foolish to stand aloof from those who are less developed, for they are our own younger brothers, learning the same lessons which we ourselves were taught only a little time before. How shortsighted to despise those who wear physical bodies of a color different from our own, for *we* have lived in that race before, and may live in it again; besides, on spiritual planes all men are one.

If we would let the truth of reincarnation sink deep into our hearts, we could no longer envy others for the qualities they possess nor lament our own limitations. Envy and lamentation alike arise from ignorance of the law by means of which those powers we admire may be made our own, if we will, not by foolish envy or idle dreaming, but by making the effort to develop them within ourselves. There is no goal so high but we may reach it by persistent effort, although many lives may be needed for the winning. There is no real failure in life except the lack of courage to try again after each apparent failure.

CHAPTER 4

THE PROCESS OF REINCARNATION

The process of reincarnation is not so simple as might be supposed, and in order to understand clearly just what takes place when a human soul is incarnated in a physical body, it is necessary to review some of the facts which have been discovered by psychical research.

A slight awakening of what is known as clairvoyant sight makes visible a delicate mist of luminous matter surrounding every living human body. This mist, usually called the aura, has been seen by thousands of people, and is now one of the commonplaces of psychical research. Usually it extends out about eighteen inches on all sides from the surface of the physical body, and in form it is egg-shaped, presenting an ovoid outline from whatever angle it may be observed. The delicate colors which sweep through it vary in hue according to the qualities of character and the habitual thoughts of the person observed, and in the same person according to the mood or thought of the moment. The colors themselves, though arranged in different areas in the aura are subject to frequent changes and modifications, because each change in consciousness is accompanied by a new vibratory wave through the matter of the aura, and each such wave has its own special color, according to the nature of the thought or feeling.

Upon going to sleep or at death the aura is withdrawn from the physical body, and it is then possible to study it by itself to see what it is like. It has been found that in the midst of the faintly-luminous ovoid is a life-size duplicate or counterpart of the physical body, which is much more prominent than the aura proper, because ninety-nine per cent of the matter of the ovoid is contained within it. Hence, after death, although the real form of the subtle body in which we are active and conscious is ovoid, nevertheless we appear exactly as we do here because of the counterpart of the physical body within the scarcely perceptible aura. We may—with a little strain upon the imagination—compare the appearance of the ovoid to one of those large glass marbles, so dear in our childhood days, in the midst of which is embedded a little man. We must imagine, however, the glass part as being ovoid in form and so delicately colored as to be scarcely visible, and picture the little man as being life size and the exact image of what we are physically. Further, we must endow the aura and image with intense vitality, and realize that our consciousness can use such a form much more easily than it can a physical body.

Additional research has shown that this luminous ovoid with its counterpart is, in reality, composed of three interpenetrating bodies, of about the same size and with very much the same arrangement of colors. They occupy the same space, the rarefied matter of which they are made intermingling with no more difficulty than either permeates dense physical matter. These three bodies of man are known as the emotional or astral body, the mental or thinking body, and the causal or soul body. In their totality they constitute the invisible ovoid by which every living human body is surrounded and interpenetrated.

In the emotional body our consciousness is expressed in the form of sensations, feelings, desires, passions, emotions. In the mental body it is expressed in the form of thoughts which can be thrown into picture-form—concrete thinking. In the soul body it is expressed in the form of thoughts which are abstract in their nature—abstract thinking. The brain itself does not generate a single thought, but is merely a sensitive instrument responding more or less to the play of consciousness in these various bodies, and the degree of the response determines the extent of our waking consciousness. Much of the activity of our consciousness working in these invisible bodies remains unreported by the brain, because of its limited power of response, and all such unrealized activity forms our subconsciousness, or, to use a better term, our superconsciousness.

When it is said that a human body is "ensouled" we ought not to get the impression that something has been put into it, like water into a vase. The relationship between the physical body and the mind is a *vibratory* one; so long as the physical body is surrounded and interpenetrated by the luminous ovoid the brain responds to the vibrations of consciousness, and we may rightly say the body is "ensouled." When, at death, the relationship is broken, it is not inapt to say that the soul has "departed." In neither case, however, has the consciousness been poured into or taken out of the physical body; the vibratory relationship alone has been broken.

After these preliminary statements it will now be possible to trace in an intelligible fashion that part of the cycle of an incarnation which commences at the death of one physical body and ends at the birth of another.

After death we find ourselves conscious and active in that part of the unseen region surrounding the earth, which is known as the astral world. Here we live for several years—usually about twenty-five—entering into the interesting activities of that world, keeping in touch with our friends whether they are physically incarnated or not, and getting rid in the meantime of any impurities which may have crept into our character during the life on earth. This part of our existence corresponds to the "paradise" of some Christian Churches and the "purgatory" of others, although in connection therewith we should rid our minds of all ideas of punishment. It is true that some people do suffer during this part of their existence, not, however, because they are being *punished*, but because of the inevitable reaction from some bad habit or wrong-doing to which they were accustomed while on earth. Further, the suffering is not forever and ever, but is only temporary and of a purifying nature. No hell exists except in the imaginations of men.

After a while, when the astral body in which we are conscious in that world has served its purpose, we sever our relationship with it—a sort of astral death—and then find ourselves vividly conscious in that portion of the unseen region known as the mental world, which corresponds to the Christian idea of "heaven." In that world we spend by far the greater part of the period between one incarnation and the next. During this portion of our existence we assimilate the experiences we gained during the previous incarnation on earth, develop into faculties and powers all the training we received, and weave into the fabric of our character all the lessons taught. This is the happiest part of the whole cycle as well as the longest, and, while we are no longer in touch directly with physical events and physical people, we are in the most sympathetic relationships with the minds of those we love and admire, which in reality is much more satisfactory than any physical relationship can ever be, because the possibilities of unhampered and joyous communion are so much greater.

Still later we cast off the radiant mind body, and then we realize our oneness with the soul, the divine Self of man. It is the soul body alone that endures and grows through all the centuries, for the physical, emotional and mental bodies are used for one incarnation only. In other words, the physical body with which we commonly identify ourselves, the emotional body which so clearly reveals our character, and the mind body with which we think, *are as we know them but for one incarnation only;* the consciousness in us which persists throughout the centuries and by which are retained all the memories of the past, is that of the soul or ego, manifested in the soul body.

It is well to remember that the life after death is by far the happiest and much the freest part of our whole existence, and that we experience no suffering whatsoever unless on earth we lived impure and unwholesome lives, or unless we cared for nothing except eating and drinking and other physical pleasures. Physical existence is really the most arduous and trying of all. This does not mean, as some people persist in thinking, that suicide is therefore desirable—for suicide is a serious mistake —but it does imply that the physical part of our existence, which many cling to so tenaciously, is the hardest part of each incarnation cycle, although it is absolutely necessary for our growth.

Before describing that part of the cycle of existence which brings us back into incarnation again, after we have realized our oneness with the soul consciousness, it will probably be helpful if a digression is made in order to explain the origin of the soul body. The story is a long one involved in many complexities, and can only be presented adequately in an advanced textbook, but we ought to be able without difficulty to grasp some of the essential points by a quick survey of the evolutionary plan.

First of all we should realize that the *whole* of Nature is living, and that every natural form, from the crystal to man, is serving as the body of a growing consciousness. We may picture wave after wave of evolving life surging up through the various kingdoms: mineral, vegetable, animal, and human. In the mineral, consciousness is scarcely awake; in the plant, it is beginning to show forth like the dislike and a faint trace of sensitiveness; in the animal, it is manifest in definite feelings, passions and desires, and in the beginnings of thought; in man, after having been subjected to the experience of hundreds of incarnations, it reaches sublime heights of spiritual understanding.

Secondly, we should realize that in the lower kingdoms consciousness evolves in the mass, while in the human kingdom there is an evolution of individuals. In the animal kingdom, as an example of mass evolution, we find that hundreds or even thousands of physical bodies of the lesser evolved animals are animated by one "group soul." As these group souls slowly develop through millions of years, they continually divide and subdivide—in a way which reminds one of the process of cell division—and after each separation of one group soul into two smaller group souls, a lesser number of animal bodies is found to be animated by each of the latter. Finally, when evolution reaches the stage where highly intelligent animals are in close contact with man, as in the case of the domesticated cat, dog and elephant, each group soul has but one animal body to represent it. A very intelligent and affectionate dog is a reincarnating entity, ready for entrance into the human kingdom, but not yet a human soul; he has a rudimentary astral and mental body, which are portion of the original group soul, but there is no soul body animated by the eternal Spirit.

The condition of an animal's mental body at this time is not wholly unlike that of an unfertilized egg; it has within it many possibilities, but it is impossible to develop them without the stimulus of a spiritual element which is as yet lacking. This element is supplied when the animal, either through intense affection for its human master, or through an act by which is sacrifices its life for a man, or through a strong mental effort to understand that which it is being taught, draws down upon itself a stream of force from the spiritual world. When this takes place a curious sort of whirlpool is set up in the heaven-world which speedily involves the mental body of the animal. When the vortex subsides a filmy and almost colorless soul body is seen and when the next incarnation takes place the physical body is human. Thus two elements enter into the human consciousness: the emotional and mental one, which had its start in the lower kingdoms—the animal in man—and a spiritual one which makes man different from any animal by giving him possibilities of growth which no animal possesses. This spiritual element is the Eternal Spirit in man, the resplendent Being, mentioned in a previous chapter, who links man to God and makes possible the divine evolution of the human race.

After this necessary digression we can now consider the process by which the soul incarnates.

At the commencement of a new incarnation, when we have exhausted our previous experience and begin to yearn for more, we draw round ourselves automatically a cloudlike mass of mental and astral matter. Out of this later on we are able to fashion our mental and emotional bodies. In the meantime we await in the astral world the formation of our new physical body, which is to be supplied by our parents. At a variable period between conception and birth we are linked with that body, and at birth our consciousness begins to function through the infant brain, but so slightly that for at least two years after birth we are unable to retain physically any memories whatsoever of what happens to us.

Although the soul of a child has had many incarnations in the past—for we are now well past the stage of evolution when many "new" souls come into incarnation—nevertheless its consciousness appears physically as that of a child for two reasons: first, its emotional and mental bodies at the beginning of an incarnation are cloudy, unorganized masses of luminous matter, and are therefore scarcely active as vehicles of consciousness; second, the physical brain of the child must be subjected to much interplay of the vibrations of consciousness and of the senses before definite areas can be specialized in the grey cells of the brain for transmitting and receiving purposes. In other words, the earlier years of a child's life are largely spent in training three instruments of consciousness: the mind body, for the expression of thoughts; the emotional body, for the expression of feelings; the physical body, for the receiving of sense impressions and for expression of the will to act. At first the aura of a child is practically colorless, but as its education proceeds the color areas begin to appear, each one signifying a trait of character or an habitual trend of thought. If the education of the child has been wisely guided, only the best of qualities will appear in the aura. If the education has been unwise or neglected many unpleasant qualities will be noticeable. The importance of education can scarcely be over-emphasized, for the value of an incarnation to the soul of the child largely depends upon it.

At the beginning of an incarnation we do not choose our parents, as a rule, because we have not knowledge enough to do so wisely. The selection of our parents, and therefore of our station and opportunities in life, is under the guidance of certain spiritual Intelligences, of whom very little is known. They have the transcendent power of surveying the whole past of every soul and selecting in complete accordance with divine justice the exact conditions of birth which every soul has earned, and in the midst of which the lessons of life can be most rapidly learned. Nothing can be more tangled than the web of human destiny, and it is not until a man has nearly completed his human evolution that he is permitted to choose the conditions of his birth for himself. Even now, however, we are indirectly influencing our relationships with others in the future, for it has been found that those who love one another are drawn together life after life in the various possible relationships: parent and child, brother and sister, lover and sweetheart, and so on. The very fact that these physical relationships are not always the same, life after life, makes possible the perfecting of the tie of love.

The sex of our physical bodies is not always the same, for the unfolding of human character can best be furthered by a series of incarnations in one sex followed by a series in the other, and so on alternately during the whole of our long evolution. The number of incarnations in any one sex ranges from one to ten and even more, but usually we have not less than three nor more than seven consecutive incarnations in one sex. The needs of our growth determine the sex of any one incarnation, since when we are born as a woman it is obvious that we develop a different set of qualities than when we are born as a man. When we have completed our human evolution our character is a magnificent blending of the virtues of both sexes.

The length of the interval between incarnations varies within wide limits, as it depends upon three factors, which in turn are variable. These are:

1. The length of the preceding earth life. A long life on earth, generally speaking, is followed by a long stay in the unseen world.

2. The intensity of the preceding earth life. Some lives are placid and uneventful, while others are crowded with varied happenings. The greater the amount of experience, the longer the interval between incarnations.

3. The level of development which has been reached in evolution. The more advanced the soul the longer the time spent in the heaven world, because the more vigorous the consciousness, the richer the meaning of every experience, and therefore the longer the time necessary to assimilate that experience.

The length of the period between incarnations has been found by actual investigation to range from five years in cases of the lowest human types to two thousand three hundred years in cases of the most developed, who still find it necessary to incarnate for the acquirement of a few remaining lessons. The general average length of interval, as said before, is about five hundred years.

Reincarnation is not an endless process, and when we have learned the lessons taught in the World-School we return no more to physical incarnation unless we come back of our own accord to act as Teachers of humanity or as Helpers in the glorious plan of evolution.

CHAPTER 5

THE PROOFS OF REINCARNATION

OBJECTIONS AND LOGICAL ARGUMENTS

The first question that occurs to a person who has listened to a discourse on reincarnation is: "What proofs have you that reincarnation is a fact?" This question is a fair one and should be answered in a satisfactory manner if the study of reincarnation is ever to command the attention of thoughtful people. Reincarnation, if true, is an evolutionary process of such importance that no effort should be spared to put the doctrine upon a solid foundation of logical argument and demonstrated fact.

Before considering the arguments in favor of reincarnation it may be well to clear out of the way a number of minor objections, so that we shall be able to examine more carefully the points worth considering at length. These objections are as follows:

Reincarnation is absurd because it claims that we can be reborn as animals. It has already been shown in an earlier chapter that the modern idea of reincarnation—and, for that matter, the original ancient teaching before it became corrupted—claims nothing of the sort; on the contrary, it affirms that the human consciousness always returns in a human body, and that, generally speaking, each new incarnation brings the person back to a slightly higher social level and amid better surroundings.

Human progress is possible without returning to this or any other planet. The idea generally current in Christian lands is that after death if we have lived up to a certain standard of morality and accepted certain theological beliefs which differ with the different Churches, we shall go to heaven and live there for ever and ever. Just what we do in heaven to while away the countless millions of years is not stated. Presumably there is some sort of progress, but just what this means is not defined. It cannot mean moral progress, as we usually understand morality, for in heaven, where there are no moral temptations, there would be no need to exercise, and hence no possibility of developing, moral strength and understanding. It cannot mean intellectual progress as we understand it here, for in heaven there would be no commercial, political, economic, social, racial or international problems upon which we could sharpen our mental faculties. There would be nothing left but metaphysical reasoning, and to many people such reasoning is not only distasteful but actually impossible. While the current idea of the heaven-life may be most pleasing to those of a devotional temperament, it is certainly not so to many others. If we could put three-fourths or even nine-tenths of the people of the world into a realm where there were no business transactions, no newspapers, books, theaters, weekends, no eating and drinking and sleeping, no manual labor, construction and invention, no painting, designing, or musical instruments, no political discussions, none of the activities and interests which stimulate the minds of men, those people would surely be unutterably bored and possibly not even conscious of their transcendental surroundings. A life for all eternity in such a heaven would stop absolutely the progress of the average man. There would be nothing to interest him or to arouse his consciousness. That which delights the man of culture is meaningless to the uncultured. Reincarnation is thoroughly logical, therefore, when it points out that the place where our mental and moral growth will be most rapid is right in the midst of physical activities and problems, around which our interests and thoughts chiefly center and not in the surroundings of a heaven remote from human life.

We may reincarnate on other planets, but not again on earth. Some people seem particularly fond of picturing the soul as wandering from planet to planet, and even from star to star, forgetting for the moment that stars are incandescent suns. They imagine, for some reason, that conditions for progress must be better elsewhere than here. This is, of course, quite uncertain, and further, even if we do assume that human beings exist on other planets, their level of development may be so different from our own, that to take incarnation there would seriously handicap our progress. There may be civilizations on other planets which are newer and consequently more backward than ours. There may also be civilizations on other planets which are more advanced than ours. If we reincarnated on the former, we should encounter such primitive conditions that our progress would not be helped; if we reincarnated on the latter we should probably be regarded as ignorant savages. Surely it is better for us in every way to reincarnate on this earth where our own development matches up with the level reached by civilization.

Notice, furthermore, that we find about us *now* people of all stages of mental and moral growth. May we not assume that they have been evolving on other planets—if the objection under discussion is a valid one—and that, therefore, on those other planets there must be about the same human inequalities that we find here? Under such circumstances, what advantage would there be in wandering from planet to planet, when all the varied conditions necessary for growth, for the savage and for the saint, are to be found on this earth? There would be none. The modern idea of reincarnation states that we are born only on this planet—during the present period of human evolution—and that we do not journey from planet to planet, except at long intervals when we go in a mass and not individually.

Reincarnation is a coldly irreligious notion. For some reason the accepted belief in a hereafter is associated in the minds of some with a lazy existence in a blissful heaven where there is nothing to do but dream gentle dreams and indulge in ecstasies of emotional exaltation. One cannot but feel at times that such ideals are only forms of spiritual selfishness. If the holding of these ideals is "warmly religious," then it must be admitted that reincarnation is "coldly irreligious," for reincarnation points out that instead of spending countless centuries idly in heaven, our greatest joy should be in learning how to make others healthier, happier, and wiser here on earth, and that our greatest privilege is to take part in hastening the spiritual unfolding of our incarnated brothers. As our own evolution progresses there will, of course, be ever greater personal happiness and understanding, but our ideal ought to be not what we can gain for ourselves, but what we can give to others. By the process of reincarnation we are brought again and again among those who need our help and can profit by our experience. Instead of seeking to save our own souls, which again is nothing but spiritual selfishness, we ought to be aflame with the ideal of human service, and regard every faculty and power we possess as hard-earned wealth to be used for the helping of others. Is this cold and irreligious? If so, then the glorious ideal of service preached by the Christ is of the same nature. Which is the nobler conception: to live for ever and ever in some idle heaven, or to return from time to time to earth to take part in the progress of the world and to help our younger brothers when they stumble and fall? Reincarnation is rich with promise and warm with the glow of consecrated service, when we realize that it means ever-increasing skill and ever-wider opportunities for the helping of man.

Reincarnation destroys the hope of recognizing friends hereafter. This statement is based upon the misconception that we are reborn immediately after death. Although in rare cases human beings are reborn almost immediately, yet in the vast majority of cases a long period is spent in the unseen realm between incarnations. While in the astral world there is no difficulty usually in finding and associating with friends in much the same way as is done here. In the heaven world, while the mode of communication is somewhat different, nevertheless we are constantly and closely in touch with those we love. And further, it should not be forgotten that whether in or out of physical incarnation the *souls* of friends are *always* in touch with one another, and that the only separation which *may* occur is here on earth during the period of an incarnation, when for some reason we do not meet physically. But even such separations are rare, for in the majority of cases we are brought into close relationship with the friends of other lives, when they and we have come back again to earth. It is the tie of love and friendship which chiefly brings souls together into family and other groups, and many a love of this life is the renewal of the love of other lives. Because reincarnation is based upon the deathless nature of the consciousness and memory of man, it does not destroy, but on the contrary, emphasizes the hope of recognizing and meeting friends hereafter.

Reincarnation brings confusion of relationship. Surely a little consideration will make clear that the priceless element in any human relationship is not the relation our physical body may hold to the physical body of another person, but the tie of affection that exists. Without affection of what moment is any relationship? Now, reincarnation makes possible the continuation and the continual enrichment of the tie of affection by a constant change in physical relationship life after life. At first thought this idea may be repellent, but after consideration we realize that no plan could be better adapted to round out and perfect the love between friends.

"When a mother first clasps her baby son in her arms that one relationship seems perfect, and if the child should die her longing would be to repossess him as her babe; but as he lives on through youth to manhood the old tie changes, and the protective love of the mother and the clinging obedience of the child merge into a different love of friends and comrades, richer than ordinary friendship from the old recollections; yet later, when the mother is aged and the son in the prime of middle life, their positions are reversed, and the son protects while the mother depends on him for guidance. Would the relation have been more perfect had it ceased in infancy with only the one tie, or is it not the richer and the sweeter from the different strands of which the tie is woven? And so with egos; in many lives they may hold to each other many relationships, and finally, standing as Brothers . . . closely knit together, may look back over past lives and see themselves in earthlife related in the many ways possible to human beings, till the cord is woven of every strand of love and duty; would not the final tie be the richer, not poorer, for the many-stranded ties?"*

Reincarnation is unknown to people in the other world. This is not entirely true, for of recent years many spiritualistic "communications" have contained information regarding reincarnation. A belief in the return of the soul has long been held by the French School of spiritualists, and is now being received with more favor in other countries. It is, however, quite true that many people in the astral world do not know of reincarnation, for the excellent reason that they do not care to know. Death does not change our consciousness at all, nor does it remove many of our prejudices, and after death we are just as apt to associate only with people who hold opinions similar to our own

---

* Annie Besant, *Death — and After?*

as we do now. If we are opposed to the idea of reincarnation before our death and refuse to examine the evidence in its favor, we usually adopt exactly the same attitude after death, even though the available evidence may be much more conclusive. It should not be forgotten that we do not have memories in the astral world of our own past lives any more than we have here, for the reason that we cannot fully remember the past until we can contact our soul consciousness, and therefore this means of verifying the truth of reincarnation is not available immediately after death.

If reincarnation were true then there could not be any increase in population. While it is true that the total population of this planet in and out of incarnation is now practically fixed numerically, because civilization has advanced too far to admit many new souls from the animal kingdom, nevertheless we ought not to lose sight of the fact that the progress of evolving beings up through all the kingdoms is a continuous one, just as a continuous stream of pupils pass through the various classes in a school. Later on, during another evolutionary cycle, a great host of reincarnating entities will graduate from the animal kingdom into the human, even as we did many thousands of years ago, but, for the time being, new pupils are not entering the World-School.

Even if the population of the world has increased, the validity of reincarnation is not imperiled, since a study of the length of the period between incarnations shows that the population of the unseen world at any one time must be many times that of the earth itself. If the population of the earth has been increased this would only mean that the population of the unseen world had been decreased proportionately, the total population of the planet remaining the same.

All logical reasoning concerning the origin of consciousness favors pre-existence, which in turn implies reincarnation. There are two principle theories with regard to human consciousness:

1. Consciousness is a by-product or result of chemical and other action in matter. This is the materialistic position and implies that consciousness is dependent upon the physical brain for existence, and that at death consciousness disappears.

2. The consciousness of man is an imperishable thing which in some way not fully understood is able to affect, and be affected by, the brain. This is often spoken of as the soul theory.

The scientific evidence was all in favor of the materialistic theory until in recent years the researches of a few psychologists and of the Theosophical Society, the Society for Psychical Research, and the Spiritualists, have uncovered a great mass of facts all pointing to the conclusion that the human consciousness survives bodily death. This evidence thoroughly substantiates the second theory and throws the materialistic conception out of court. It should also be noted that the evidence, when carefully studied as a whole, shows that the human consciousness loses none of its mental, moral, and spiritual qualities by the death of the physical body, and hence that these qualities could not have been the product of bodily heredity or cellular structure. The soul theory, therefore, is the only one which may be held by one who does not disregard scientific evidence. Of the soul theory there are two versions:

(a) The conscious personality is brought into existence at birth. This may be spoken of as special creation.

(b) The conscious personality existed before birth. This is known as preexistence.

The first version, that of special creation, is the one commonly accepted in Christian thinking, although it leads to conclusions of which its exponents are seemingly unaware. In the first place, to think of human parents, by means of a physical act, creating an *immortal* personality, is to suppose a logically impossible thing. A consciousness which comes into *existence* by the physical process of reproduction will surely cease to exist by the physical process of death. That which has a beginning in time cannot be exempt from dissolution in time. Or, as Hume puts it in philosophical language: "What is incorruptible must be ungenerable." In the second place, if we claim that some *divine* power creates the soul at birth, it is rather difficult to explain why the exercise of that power is dependent upon the sexual passion of man.

Third, if each soul is created at birth, why are the mental, moral, and spiritual qualities so different in different people, ranging from the ignorance and immorality of the savage to the wisdom and morality of the saint? Inasmuch as these qualities of mind and character are found to exist after physical death they must obviously be aspects of the consciousness of the soul as they share its immortality. Fourth, if each soul comes to earth for the first time at birth, having been created with its physical body, how can we explain the enormous differences in the destiny of each?

All logical reasoning is in favor of the preexistence of the soul, with the associated idea of reincarnation, for we can then explain that the differences between people are due to the difference in soul-age, that the destiny of each soul is the resultant of the past, and that the physical process of reproduction and birth supplies the soul with a physical body, but does not in any way determine its existence.

One life only on earth is purposeless in millions of cases. Those who hold that we live but once on earth seldom realize how lacking in purpose such a life would be in many millions of cases. If each human being lived for some sixty or seventy years and met with experiences of various kinds, we might logically assume that that life had some important bearing upon the progress of the soul after death, even though we might not understand just how a taste of physical existence could hasten the advancement of a spiritual being. But, as we know full well, millions of children, instead of growing to maturity, die after a few months or even hours of life. Of what value to an immortal soul are a few hours of existence in the form of a half-conscious babe? Or even if the child does live longer, but is reared, as so many millions are, in the vice-ridden slums of a great city, what is the underlying purpose of it all if earth is visited but once?

If, however, we live a series of lives on earth and each incarnation is a continuation of the preceding one, then even a short life may serve some purpose. Even a few unlovely years are not devoid of meaning when we realize that in the body of that child a comparatively undeveloped soul is learning such primitive lessons of right and wrong as it can at present assimilate. The underlying principle is that nothing is ever lost, nothing forgotten, and however short a life may be, it either adds something of value to the memories of the soul, or permits the payment of some hampering debt.

Is it not irrational to take for granted, as so many do, that after a single incarnation the soul never again returns to earth, although on earth countless lessons are offered which would be of the utmost value to that soul? Why should he not come back, and, for that matter, why should not *we* return, even though our own experience has been so much wider? Is there nothing more on earth for us to learn? Lessing clearly saw the need for reincarnation when he wrote: "Why should

I not come back as often as I am capable of acquiring fresh knowledge, fresh expertness? Do I bring away so much from once that there is nothing to repay the trouble of coming back?"

Even if we do live a long physical life of many opportunities and are unusually diligent we can gain only a little knowledge of the treasures of the world. But, small as our understanding of the world may be under such circumstances, it is large compared to the knowledge of the average man. After a limited education he goes into business, marries, settles down, has children, and then finds himself forced to work constantly just to keep the pot boiling and the home comfortable. He usually finds time to read his paper and may occasionally study a little, but there are always unlimited fields of knowledge which it is a physical impossibility for him to traverse. Science, philosophy, religion, art, history, language, literature, may appeal to him variously according to his temperament, but however strong the appeal, he is forced by his physical and mental limitations to forego everything with the possible exception of some tiny phase of human endeavor. No human mind ever existed that was able to grasp in a single incarnation more than a fragment or two of all that there is to know; this fact we must face squarely if we hold to the assumption that we live but once on earth.

By means of reincarnation, however, there is not one field of knowledge we may not explore, there is not one great civilization whose genius we may not study first-hand, there is not one human activity in which we may not share. In the long history of our soul's growth we have lived in many an ancient city, we have witnessed and taken part in great events, we have met some of the famous characters of the past, and in the lives to come ever greater richness of experience awaits us. There is no hurry, unless we are eager to train ourselves so that we may the sooner be able wisely to help others, and under any circumstances it is well to take time to master thoroughly each phase of life as it comes to us. Then, when the time comes for graduation from the World-School, we shall be proficient in many lines and wise in all.

Reincarnation makes possible the attainment of perfection. "Be ye therefore perfect" has long seemed almost like mockery to man. What chance have we to become perfect in one short life? Even worldly success seems far beyond our reach oftentimes, for when we contrast ourselves with other human beings who have already won their way to honor in the realms of science, art, philosophy, or religion, we cannot but realize most keenly our own limitations. Christlike perfection? It is an ideal so far beyond the possibilities of the average man that it never enters his head to try to attain it. He may talk about it vaguely, but he does not attempt to live it. Reincarnation, however, brings the ideal of perfection within reach, for reincarnation means unlimited opportunity, and opportunity implies growth and final attainment.

Reincarnation illuminates the problem of evil.
To think of God as being good, loving, just, and all-powerful, and the same time explain why the world should be filled with misery, sorrow, and injustice, has been a problem so troublesome that philosophers and theologians have been unable to solve it. The reason has been that they either ignored or did not know of reincarnation. Let us see what light reincarnation casts upon this problem.

Within each soul at the beginning of its incarnations are latent all the moral, intellectual, and spiritual qualities which later it will show forth. By the process of reincarnation, which brings each soul back again and again into the activities and problems of daily life, these qualities are slowly awakened one by one. *Until they are so awakened,* however, human beings are unmoral, unintelligent, unspiritual. Tersely put, the so-called "evil" qualities of man are due to the *unawakened* state of the opposite good qualities. If we are cruel it is because we have not yet awakened compassion. If we are selfish it is because we have not yet awakened unselfishness. When a good quality is aroused the "evil" quality disappears, for "evil" is not a positive thing in itself but only the absence of the good. A little child is often terribly cruel to an animal, inflicting pain without the slightest idea that it is doing wrong. A few years later, when the mature soul of the child is able more fully to express itself in the youthful emotional body, the child is no longer cruel. The same principle applies in the greater evolution of the soul. Where a good quality has not yet been aroused to expression there is found an evil; we are ignorant until experience has taught us wisdom; we are morally weak until we have developed moral strength.

When we learn to regard the world as a school, and realize that every living thing upon it is being taught, not by precept but by experience, the problem of evil takes on a new aspect. Surely it is obvious that if we are to possess any judgment whatsoever between right and wrong we must have gained it by having in the past chosen the wrong and learned from the results which followed that it was wrong. To be told that an act is wrong does not really convince us, although for a time we may refrain from that act. *But when we suffer as the consequence of that act*, the conviction is absolute. In the World-School we learn what is right by being permitted to do what is wrong; in no other way can a knowledge of right and wrong be obtained.

Reincarnation is in conformity with the economy of Nature. If the purpose of physical life is the gaining of experience, as it undoubtedly must be, then the economy of Nature would suggest that human beings trained in the affairs of the world would be reborn in the world where they can make the best use of their knowledge and training. Of what particular use in heaven will be much of the technical knowledge we have gained on earth? Yet such knowledge, especially if it keeps on accumulating life after life in the form of *expert faculty*, will be of the greatest value in the physical world. If the great men in science and invention, in politics and statesmanship, in music and painting, in religion and spiritual wisdom, *are great because of experience gathered during many a past incarnation*, have we not a magnificent argument in favor of the ultimate perfection of humanity and of civilization? Civilizations may perish, and with them their arts and sciences, their religions and their philosophies, but the human beings who molded those civilizations do not perish—they live and remember and after a time they return again to earth, endowed with the expert faculties gained in the past, to share in the building up of new and more beautiful civilizations.

Reincarnation explains the rise and fall of nations. To the student of history there is something very suggestive in the extraordinary way in which nations rise to world-power, enjoy a period of prosperity, and then sink to obscurity. The external conditions alone are not sufficient cause for the rapid decay which sometimes takes place, as in the case of the past history of Spain. When only mediocre leaders appear, when the populace no longer responds to heroic ideals, when the birth-rate begins to decline, nothing, seemingly, can be done to stop the swift descent. Why is this?

The greatness of a nation depends upon the opportunities offered by it to incoming souls. If the physical heredity of a nation is comparatively free from social diseases, if the educational facilities and the religious instruction provided are good, if the acts of the government are based more upon moral ideals than selfish ends, then it would seem to follow that the human egos born in that nation are likewise of an advanced moral character. In short, the achievements of a nation depend upon the development of the souls taking incarnation in it, which in turn depends upon what is offered those souls. National righteousness and wholesome educational facilities form the greatest attractions. A nation begins to decay when the most advanced egos are attracted elsewhere, for, when greatness is no longer available, perforce younger and therefore less experienced souls must take the reins of government and uphold the national standards. Each nation, like a class in school, teaches certain lessons and qualities by means of its social, moral, and political standards, and hence the lowering of these standards means a change in the quality of pupil. The higher the national standards, the mightier becomes the nation. When Rome became morally rotten and politically corrupt the egos who had made Rome great began to be born among the less civilized but physically purer Teutonic peoples, with the inevitable result that Rome decayed while the younger nations flourished.

Reincarnation explains the reappearance of the characteristics of earlier races. When we study the temperamental characteristics of different nations in the mass they seem in a most singular way to reflect the spirit of certain ancient civilizations. There is a close resemblance, for example, between the British Empire, as it was, and that of ancient Rome. In the English people particularly we can notice the same tendency towards colonization, the same lawmaking instinct, the same thoroughness in every undertaking, the same massive style of architecture, the same sacrificing of beauty to utility and strength, and, it must be confessed, the same lack of imagination in art, religion and philosophy.

In France, on the contrary, the racial characteristics in the mass remind one very much more of ancient Greece. There is the same imaginative touch, the same love of beauty, the same worship of form and expression, the same intellectual keenness, and the same changeableness. Naturally there is a sprinkling of the Greek temperament in England and of the Roman temperament in France, but in the main the characteristics are as described. Why? May it not be that in a mass the egos of Greece have taken incarnation in France, the egos of Rome in England?

This reversion to earlier racial temperaments is seen most strikingly in individuals. Surely Keats could have been no other than the reincarnation of some poet of ancient Greece, while the craftsmanship of the old Roman historians can be detected in Macaulay, Hume, and Gibbon. The spirit of the Vedantin philosophy of India reappears in the works of Hegel, Fichte, and Kant, while Schopenhauer was apparently recalling much of the philosophy of Buddhism gained in another life. It has been well said that "whenever the deeper layers of a man's being are offered to the world in some creation through philosophy, literature, art, or science, there may be noted tendencies started in other lives."*

Reincarnation explains the appearance of great men in groups. When we study the chronological appearance of those men who have materially helped the progress of the arts and sciences, of philosophy and religion, it is interesting to note that they apparently come in groups, and that oftentimes within the groups there are certain common characteristics. This is especially noticeable among the artists. Botticelli, Michelangelo, Titian, Raphael, and Holbein form a chronological group. Immediately after come Rubens, Velasquez, Rembrandt, Carlo Dolci, and Murillo. A little time elapses and then are born Hogarth, Reynolds, Gainsborough, Romney, and Raeburn, who are followed later by Watts, Holman Hunt, Rosetti and Millais. The founders of modern music were also born in the same singular way. First came Handel and Bach, then Mendelssohn, Mozart and Beethoven, and lastly, in quick succession, a large group composed of Schubert, Chopin, Schumann, Liszt, Wagner, Rubenstein, Brahms, and Grieg. The appearance of an isolated group of American poets and philosophers is also suggestive, particular-

* G. F. Moore, *Metempsychosis, p.* 70.

ly as they were born together in one section of the United States, and many of them, later on, became intimate friends. The members of this group were Bryant, Emerson, Longfellow, Whittier, Poe, Thoreau, Whitman, and Lowell, to mention the most important.

Is there not inspiration in the thought that life after life groups of intimate friends and co-workers incarnate together to continue their activities? Is there not joy in the idea that we shall labor together in the future to make this old world happier and more beautiful? Is there not hope and consolation in the assurance that the strains of a Beethoven, the artistic mastery of a Raphael, the philosophy of an Emerson are not lost to the world, but will be given again to mankind in some later civilization, with even greater skill and understanding, by the same egos who before won the admiration of the world?

Reincarnation and a divine moral order are inseparable. The most baffling philosophical problem with which scholar and priest have struggled for centuries is the apparent injustice of the circumstances of life. Is there any moral power or law guiding the destinies of men? If there is, then why do not good actions always bring happiness and success, wrong actions suffering and failure? Seemingly they do not, for sometimes the most innocent act leads to the most dire result, goodness is often repaid by suffering, while deliberate wrongs go unpunished. Very rarely, seemingly, does "the punishment fit the crime."

Notice also how there is much injustice in the circumstances in which we find ourselves placed at birth. How much depends upon our nationality, parentage, physical and mental capacities, our early training, yet apparently these circumstances are quite out of our power to control. We must accept whatever destiny gives us, yet how fickle and purposeless that destiny sometimes seems! Sometimes we are pampered, sometimes starved; sometimes we are allowed to play, sometimes forced to work; but underlying it all we cannot detect any moral purpose at work. So much bitter injustice seems to run through the whole of life, that we really cannot be blamed for doubting the words of a preacher who tries to tell us that an all-knowing God watches over everything.

The root of the difficulty lies not in the actual injustice of life itself, but in our unconscious assumption, while looking at life, that we come but once to earth. Naturally, when we attempt to justify the events of one incarnation, considered as an isolated existence without any past causes to explain it, we cannot do so. It would be just as impossible to understand how a pupil in one of our schools had the power to read and write, if we chose to ignore the days he had previously spent in school developing that power.

Reincarnation brings with it the assurance that there is a moral law constantly operative in the universe by pointing out that our individual destinies are self-made. Our mental capacities, moral character, physical well-being, and every important event of each incarnation, are the results of our own actions, desires, and thoughts in the other incarnations; hence destiny is not a thing imposed from without by some arbitrary Power, but the accumulated results of past causes. Everyday examples of this same principle readily occur to us. If a boy will not study at school and therefore grows up an ignorant man, his ignorance is due not to some imposed destiny, but is the direct result of his own willfulness. If a youth, in sowing his wild oats, contracts some dread disease which does not make its appearance until many years later, he is not being punished for his previous wrong-doing, but is suffering from the results of his earlier mistakes. From the suffering he grows wiser and learns his lesson, which is always the purpose underlying suffering.

This is the angle from which we should approach the study of human destiny. We may think of the moral law as one of action followed by reaction, each cause always producing a certain effect, every effect always having a preceding cause. Our past actions are reacting upon us now in the form of physical environment and circumstances; our past thoughts are the builders of our character; our past desires are determining our present opportunities. Nothing merely happens in the moral world any more than in the physical. We are what we are to-day by what we have done, thought, and desired in the past, not only during other lives on earth, but during the earlier years of this life.

Whatever comes to us of weal or woe is the rebound of a force started by ourselves. It may be that some person with whom we come in contact is the *agent* for bringing about the result, but we are always ultimately responsible. This conception of destiny is in perfect agreement with everyday common sense. If, in daily life, a man persists in making sarcastic remarks about others, he becomes thoroughly disliked. He is not being punished by being disliked, but he is only learning the universal law that every cause has its appropriate effect. Apply this same idea to everything which happens to us, and we shall understand clearly the reincarnational interpretation of destiny.

If each man's destiny is self-made there can be no injustice, and it can only be self-made if reincarnation is a fact. Either destiny is due to divine caprice or to mere physical chance, which reduces the world of events to moral chaos; or it is due to causes set going by ourselves, which implies reincarnation. Moral order and reincarnation are inseparable, and only when we realize that we have lived and are now living a series of lives on earth, each one linked up with all the others which have gone before, are we able to see how God is just and that purpose governs every phase of existence and experience. What happens to us is not in any sense a punishment, but a result, and the underlying purpose of it all is to teach us by actual experience what is right and wrong, wise and unwise.

Recall to mind for the moment the case of the man released from a prison, referred to in an earlier chapter, and let us imagine how the minister of the Gospel could have spoken to him had reincarnation still been retained as a Christian teaching.

"Brother," we may think of him as saying, "you have suffered this incarnation for a terrible wrong you did another man in a past life. In that life you deliberately allowed an innocent man to go to prison in order to save yourself, and now you have learned that what you did was wrong and terribly unjust, because you yourself have suffered the same fate. How else could you have been brought to see your mistake, for in that past life you thought yourself exceedingly clever and rejoiced that you had escaped punishment. You have suffered terribly in this life, but now you know that in God's universe not one wrong can be done without full payment. Never again will you be cruel to another as you were before, thinking only of yourself and not of his sufferings, for you have been the helpless victim of similar cruelty and realize that it is a violation of the Law of Love. I know how hard has been the learning of that lesson, and I realize how much you have endured, but lift up your head and face the world with renewed courage, for you have paid forever that terrible debt of the past, and you are now free to go forward into a new life. Let me help you, and with Christ's Love your life shall be made useful and happy again. Even though this incarnation may have been marred as the inevitable result of your past mistake, nevertheless the years and the lives to come lie now in the hollow of your hand to make of them what you will. Let the past be past, look only to the future, and you will see the dawning of a better day."

The results of all that we do in one life cannot be worked out immediately. Is it not obvious that in the short span of a single life on earth we cannot repay all the physical and moral debts we have contracted? We act and think and desire up to the very last moments of our physical life, and if, in so doing, we have injured others, how and where can adjustment be made? In heaven? It is difficult to see how in a spiritual world due recompense can be made for a physical act. In many cases the doer of the act is ignorant that he has done wrong; he is morally blind because of lack of experience. He might be forced to make some sort of amends hereafter in heaven by being asked to feel sorry about it, or to say that he did wrong, or to burn— as some people think—in the fires of hell, but would any of these punishments really *educate* him or in any way *compensate* for the physical act? From the viewpoint of reincarnation each debt for which we obligate ourselves must be paid in kind: a physical wrong must be repaid physically so that we may learn not to make a similar mistake in the future, a moral wrong must be repaid by suffering moral ill so that we may understand the working of the law. Adequate compensation is possible only if reincarnation is a fact.

Reincarnation explains the enigmas of heredity.
It has been stated by some that reincarnation
ignores heredity. On the contrary, it explains many
of its problems. The laws of heredity are still very
obscure and it is not clear to scientists how qualities
are transmitted—if at all—from parents to offspring. In the lower kingdoms the offspring so
closely resemble the parents that little difficulty is
experienced in formulating a set of laws; but in
the human kingdom, while physical traits, characteristics, and appearances may be transmitted, it
has proved most puzzling to explain the great
mental and moral differences which frequently are
found.

The answer given by reincarnation is that while
we get our physical bodies from our parents, we,
as reincarnating egos, bring with us our mental and
moral characteristics. Thus, any human being is
an intimate blend of the physical qualities derived
from his parents, and of non-physical qualities re-
sulting from his own past experience. Children
born of feebleminded or vicious parents are often
immoral or weak mentally, first, because of the poor
quality of the physical bodies, and second, because
of the undeveloped egos drawn to take birth
through such parents. If we supplement the facts
of physical heredity by the facts of reincarnation
we get a true and singularly illuminating picture
of the whole process of evolution.

Reincarnation explains the mental and moral dif-

ferences between people. How can we explain logically, except by reincarnation, the enormous mental and moral differences between people? Let us, for the sake of illustration, imagine four men standing in a row.

The first man may be grossly ignorant, amoral, and because of his highly simplistic way of life, difficult to teach so that he falters before the slightest intellectual problem. Something more than mere brain-structure is needed for real thinking.

Beside him, we will suppose, there stands a professor in mathematics, equipped with a mind as keen and as swift as a rapier in dealing with mental problems. What makes the difference between the two men? According to current religious ideas the souls of the two men are identical, although it is evident that mentally they are widely different. Is the difference due to physical heredity, as is claimed by the scientists? If so, then we are quite justified in assuming that after death, when the soul is released from the physical body and therefore exists in a realm where physical heredity is no longer operative, the mental ability of the professor and the mental inability of the savage will both have disappeared, leaving—what? Some sort of soul-consciousness which is not mental, and therefore of which we cannot form the slighest conception? But we know, from the positive results of psychical research, that the mind of a professor after death is as different from that of a savage as it was before death. Hence we have every reason for concluding that what we call mental power is one of the aspects of the consciousness of the soul, and that therefore the development of the ego of the professor is vastly greater than that of the man with the newer ego. This, of course, distinctly implies reincarnation as the only means by which this evolutionary difference could be brought about.

Let us assume that the third man is quite quick-witted but unscrupulous; eager to make money regardless of the morality of the transaction. This man impresses one with the extent of his cunning but not with the quality of his character.

Contrast such a type with our fourth man, a saint in the fullest meaning of the word, gifted with the most delicate sense of honor, with a fine perception of right and wrong, with the most wonderful ideal of service. Are the souls of these two men identical? If so, then the materialistic scientists are right, and the immorality of the one and the morality of the other are only the results of differing physical heredity and training. By the same sort of reasoning we can also reach the strange conclusion that the honor, the moral purity, the spirit of sacrifice found in one, but lacking in the other, must disappear at death because such qualities are due only to physical hereditary causes. This is obviously absurd, for if human life is to have any meaning whatsoever, moral and spiritual qualities must also be aspects of the soul-consciousness, and if at birth these qualities are widely different it must imply a difference in souls.

The fundamental idea of reincarnation is that the differences we see around us among human beings are due not to any divine favoritism or to the blind working of any law of physical heredity, but to the difference in soul age. Every capacity of mind, every ability of hand, every quality of heart, were not bestowed upon us as gifts but earned by hard labor. No one can give us character; it must be self-evolved in the school of life.

CHAPTER 6

THE PROOFS OF REINCARNATION

THE MEMORY OF PAST LIVES

The existence of memories. However convincing may be the logical arguments in favor of reincarnation, we must not ignore the fact that its final proof depends upon our power to remember our past lives. To many people the strongest argument against reincarnation is contained in the question: "If we have lived before on earth why do we not remember our past lives?" They point out that not only is the truth of reincarnation involved in the apparent absence of all memories, but also the moral justification of the process of rebirth itself. Why should we suffer *now* the consequences of acts performed in other lives when we retain not the slightest memory of those acts? As Moore remarks: "The objection was long ago urged by Epicurus against the Pythagorean doctrine, that, inasmuch as the soul has no memory of former existences, and there is no conscious personal identity run-

ning through the series of rebirths, the consequences fall virtually upon another, who knows not
the cause and cannot be made wiser or better by the
punishment he bears."

If there are no memories of the past, and therefore no way for the soul to learn from its destiny
by matching effect with cause, then most certainly
reincarnation is meaningless, and the whole process
of evolution a cruel and futile torment. Not only
the validity of the theory of reincarnation but the
moral character of the evolutionary process itself
centers round the brief question: "Do memories
exist?" If they do, then reincarnation is true; if
they do not, then reincarnation is not true.

The first step to take in answering this all-
important question is to determine in what form
memories of *this* life are retained. Then, with a
clear understanding of the working of memory in
one life we can apply such tests as will show whether
we retain now any memories of past lives, thus
proving or disproving the truth of reincarnation.

We find, probably to our surprise that the memories we have now of the earlier years of this life are
quite different from what we usually suppose. In
the first place, the first three or four years of our
existence have been entirely blotted out from
memory, yet we know we must have been alive and
conscious during those years because we are alive
and conscious now. We have not the slightest personal proof of the matter, however, so far as memory goes. In the next place, we notice that practi-

cally all memories of the *details* of the past have disappeared. This is true not only of the earlier years of this life, but of this year, this week, yesterday. Even at the end of a day few people can recall exactly what they did during that day, much less remember what they said and thought. Evidently, then, the brain is enabling us to forget great masses of details—indeed this may be one of the important functions of the brain.

Of all the experiences through which we have gone, of all the thoughts which have thronged our brains, what remains? Summaries only, and it is by these summaries alone that we know we have gone through the detailed experiences. An example or two will show exactly what is meant by "summary."

We read easily, but in the act of reading we have not the slightest memory of the thousands of ways and places in which we learned the meaning and grammatical arrangement of the printed letters beneath our eyes. We know that in the past we learned the meaning of the words, not because we recall the details, which make possible the act of reading, but because *we can read*. The possession of that faculty is the sole proof that we have encountered a great mass of experience in the past. We have many such faculties at our command.

We are very careful now not to put our fingers into boiling water. Why? Not because we have been scalded recently, but because many years ago at a time out of reach of our brain-memories, we suffered when we thrust inquisitive but ignorant fingers into boiling water. We have completely forgotten that early experience, but we know we must have gone through such an episode because of our present tendency to be careful. Such a tendency is a summary of past experience, and we have hundreds of such tendencies controlling our actions.

We would not now under any circumstances be guilty of a lie. It would be against our honor and contrary to every instinct. Yet, while young, we told lies and were punished for them. We lied again and again, in the artless way of childhood, until, through the countless lessons of the home, we realized that lying was wrong. The detailed memories of those punishments and lessons have disappeared, but the trait of character remains. There are many such traits, some good and some bad, which are instinctive in us.

These examples indicate clearly what is taking place all the time in our daily lives. We encounter masses of details which we forget, but from those details we extract certain rules of life and conduct, certain faculties, powers, tendencies, which are of the utmost value to us. The details by themselves would be an enormous handicap for they would only encumber our minds, but the summaries are valuable because they are always available for immediate use.

Turning now to the consideration of reincarnation, is it possible to find any memory-summaries which indicate that we have lived on earth before?

Obviously it will be necessary to study with special care the characteristics of children, since, theoretically, it is in the child-mind that such memories will most clearly be seen. It may be that we are already fully acquainted with the existence of such summaries, but have not recognized them as memories of past lives because our attention has never been drawn before to reincarnation. Let us see the various forms taken by these possible memories of past lives.

Innate faculties of children. Have we never been struck by the mental and moral differences between children? Even in the same family, and sometimes in the case of twins where the prenatal conditions are the same, the children are very different. One child turns instinctively towards art, and desires nothing better than to be permitted to spend hours with crayon and paper. Another is always building things and, when older, haunts every place where manufacturing is done. A third shows much shrewdness in trade, and as soon as possible, even to the neglect of school, secures a business position. A fourth is a dreamy student, caring more for a book than the hurry of life. The types of children are many and are most puzzling to the students of heredity, because in so many cases the characteristics of the children do not match up either with those of the parents or of more remote relations. Further, these innate tendencies show forth very early in life, and oftentimes in the midst of hostile conditions.

May it not be that the innate qualities of a child indicate quite clearly the general lines along which the soul of that child has been trained in previous incarnations, and that every such quality is in reality a memory-summary?

It is not wholly illogical, for example, to suppose that if a soul had been interested in music in the past and a musician for several lives, any sort of musical instruction would easily be grasped at the beginning of a new incarnation, and further, that such a soul would surely be drawn to incarnation in a family of musicians so that it might be provided not only with the proper sort of education but also with a physical body of sufficient delicacy and nervous response. It is also within reason that if no interest had been taken in music during any past incarnation no amount of education in this life could arouse that interest to any extent. This argument will surely appeal to teachers of music, if to no one else, for all too frequently they are expected to transform human clods into musicians.

When, from the inner world, we are linked to an infant body in order to commence another day in the great World-School, we do not bring with us from the viewpoint of reincarnation full memories of the aeonic past through which we have lived—for no human brain is sufficiently responsive to reproduce the knowledge of the soul—but a set of innate faculties which sum up, in a form ready for instant use in the emergencies of life, all the experiences through which we have gone. Thus our innate faculties indicate the interests and activities of other incarnations.

The knowledge we gain is therefore never lost, even physically, so far as its *practical* application is concerned. The boy who knows instinctively how to handle tools as soon as they are placed in his hands has been a skilled artisan in the past; the youth who becomes the recognized leader of his playmates and inspires them to fight valiantly in mimic battles, is an old warrior come back in a young body; the dreamy child who understands the language of the rustling forest and the restless sea, and whose heart overflows with rapture in the presence of beauty, reveals the poet or artist of earlier centuries; the young man who loves the excitement of the market-place and enjoys the checkered game of loss and gain, is but showing traits of character engrained when a merchant in other lands; the lad whose whole nature yearns for spiritual things and is stirred to the depths by religious ceremonials, tells us of priestly avocations in the past.

The maternal instinct. The maternal instinct is very common in girls, and is sometimes found in boys. Has it never occurred to us that a child playing with dolls is dimly recalling memories of other lives when the loving care of babies was an actual experience? Indeed, all instincts can be explained logically in the light of reincarnation. Why should a chick, just hatched from the egg, run hastily for shelter when the shadow of a hawk flits over the ground? Instinct, we call it, but merely to name a thing does not explain it. But if in the instinct of the chick we see the working of a memory which sums up many a death in the past by hawks, we have found an explanation.

The capacity to see a truth. A new truth is presented to two people of equal education and intellectual power. One grasps it immediately, the other cannot see it. Another new truth is presented to the same two people, and this time the positions are reversed—the first cannot understand, the second is inspired. Is there any more logical explanation than that an immediate understanding of a truth, no matter how incompletely it may have been presented, shows that that truth had been met with before and understood during a previous incarnation? There is much to support the statement that we never accept an absolutely new truth and that when one appeals to us at sight it is evidence that we have encountered it before.

The power to generalize from a single experience. Some people are able, especially those who are intuitive, to formulate a universal law of experience upon the basis of a single episode. That single experience, which leaves other people no wiser than before, seems to call up in them whole vistas of moral understanding and a most mature power of judgment. Why should some people be gifted in this way? How is it possible for a woman of the greatest refinement, who knows little of the darker side of life, to be able to advise her children so wisely? Not all mothers are able to do this, but

some can and do. From what well of experience do
they draw their water of knowledge of good and
evil? Intuition, it is sometimes called, but surely
what is such intuition but the voice of past experience? Surely, also, the wide understanding which
occasionally comes to one who has passed through
some sorrow or some trial, and whose heart
opens out to realize the sorrows and trials of all
men, is not due to an inexplicable gift but is the
result of an uprush of memory-summaries of the
past.

The capacity to understand unknown experience.
The power displayed by some authors and speakers
to understand experience through which they themselves have not gone in this life is most significant.
One of the most curious cases is that of William
Sharp, who, though of a most masculine temperament, wrote under the name of Fiona Macleod as
only a woman could write. Or take the case of a
dramatist, such as the author of the Shakespeare
plays, entering with such fidelity and understanding into the feelings of a Macbeth, the moods of a
Hamlet, the sorrows of a King Lear, the revels of
a Falstaff. Could this extraordinary insight into the
intricacies of human nature be gained in any other
way than by actually having lived through such
conditions in the past and being able, *in feeling*, to
re-live that past?

Aspiration greater than ability. How frequently
the aspiration of a man is greater than his ability!
He tries eagerly to achieve some end but fails piti-

fully. His mind outruns the capacity of his brain, his longings outstrip his powers. If physical heredity were the only factor to be considered this would hardly be the case, for the mind, brought into existence by the brain, could not be greater than the brain. Surely, in this case, the aspirations are due to actual achievements in past lives, made impossible in this life because of limitations imposed by neglect of opportunities. In other words, a faculty to be kept in working order must be used; if we neglect it in one life and let our opportunities slip by, then in the next life we are handicapped by physical inability though still possessed of the inner faculty.

The consciousness of a child recapitulates the past. The curious changes which take place in the consciousness of a child have been frequently commented upon. Many children when quite young are veritable little savages, heartless, cruel, and selfish. As they grow older they enter into what may be called the barbarian stage of existence, during which they revel in fighting and foolish "dares." After a while this gives way to a more civilized point of view. Some children mature early and others late, the degree of maturity varying within wide limits. Some children are old men at ten, others are frolicsome boys at forty.

The scientific explanation of these changes is that the child recapitulates, or quickly lives over again, the whole of the *physical* evolutionary past. The reincarnational explanation is that the child relives quickly the whole series of its own past lives, which is more logical, because we are dealing with changes in consciousness and not merely growth of cell-structures.

Propensity to vice or virtue. In many children the best of parents and the most careful training are unable to prevent the emergence of vicious tendencies, while in other children criminal parents and vile surroundings cannot stop the unfolding of virtuous tendencies. The propensity to vice or virtue is most logically explained as a memory-summary carried over from the last life and aroused again to activity in the new environment with the awakening of consciousness. The voice of conscience itself is really the memory of past decisions regarding right and wrong, and so it is that a savage has little conscience because his past experience has been so slight.

Genius and infant precocity. One of the most easily recognizable forms of the memory of past lives is genius. It is so unique, such a sudden dawning not to be accounted for by any law of heredity, that it grips our attention immediately. The family in which a genius is born is usually ordinary, with little of promise even throughout the whole of the ancestry. The offspring of a genius are seldom noteworthy, for genius seemingly does not possess the power to transmit itself. Hence we are driven to the conclusion that the emergence of genius in a family has little to do with physical heredity.

From the viewpoint of reincarnation, genius results when a soul of wide experience along a certain line—mathematics, music, painting—is brought into incarnation in a physical body of exceptional sensitiveness. Because of the past experience a genius can do with ease what another man, though possessing real ability, can accomplish only after much labor and many failures.

"The manifestation of any capacity . . . depends on two indispensable factors: first, an ego or consciousness who has developed that capacity by repeated experiments in past lives; and second, a suitable instrument, a physical body, of such nature structurally as makes possible the expression of that faculty."*

Masculine women and feminine men. A not uncommon feature of our modern civilization is a type of human being in whom the character and mentality do not seem to fit the sex of the physical body. Some women are thoroughly masculine in their reasoning, attitude towards life, and even in their dress, while some men are emotional, intuitive, and effeminate in dress. An acceptable explanation is that supplied by reincarnation, which is that the soul is born now in a body of one sex and now in a body of the other, for the purpose of gaining a rounded-out education. After a series of lives in masculine bodies with the accompanying experience which is the portion of men, it is obvious that when a change of sex occurs decided masculine traits will remain even though the physical body

* C. Jinarajadasa, *How We Remember Our Past Lives.*

be feminine. In the same way, a soul who had been learning the lessons of a woman for several incarnations could not suddenly adopt the masculine point of view merely because of a change of physical body. In brief, our temperament is largely a summation of the memories of the past.

Unaccountable fears. Psychologists have been much occupied of late in studying the strange fears and fancies which at times boil up from the subconscious levels of the mind, and assert themselves against the force of the will. One explanation is that they are due to prenatal influences unconsciously exerted by the mother on the unborn child. Another explanation offered is that they are suppressed and forgotten fears of early childhood.

From the reincarnational viewpoint they are half-memories of some terrifying event which took place in a previous life: the fear of water, for example, being due to a death by drowning; the fear of fire to a death by burning, and so on.

Sudden friendships. Another interesting form of memory is that revealed in sudden friendships. Two people meet for the first time, and the moment they clasp hands or even catch sight of one another, a swift intuitive friendship springs up which time can neither diminish nor improve. It is not all a matter of temperament, as some have claimed, for in many cases the two people are very different in their personal and other characteristics.

In the light of reincarnation such friendships mean that two dear friends of a previous incarnation have met one another for the first time this life. The mutual trust, the quick sympathy and ready understanding, the loving sacrifice which distinguish such friendships, are the results of many lives of friendship in the past, during which the tie of affection grew ever stronger and more perfect.

Two people who have loved one another in the past cannot be kept apart. They are drawn together life after life, and the relationship continually becomes more beautiful. Each life, as they meet for the first time, there is a sudden leaping up of that flame of love and trust which tells of many a meeting in the past. When a friendship like this comes into one's life it truly compensates for many of the hardships with which physical existence is associated.

The feeling of having known a place before. This is an experience so common that it is often one of the first arguments advanced in favor of reincarnation. A man goes to a strange city, but upon walking the streets feels curiously at home, and at times is even able to anticipate what will be seen upon the next turning of the road. There may be a sense of unfamiliarity about many of the new structures, but the old buildings have all the feeling about them of familiar landmarks.

Another variation of this same sort of memory is the vivid sensation which sweeps over a man upon reaching a country for the first time of having "come home." It is just as if one were returning to one's own country after a long absence. Some have felt this upon visiting England, Italy, Greece, Egypt, or India. The sensation was not due to the amount of reading they had done about these countries, for in a number of cases very little reading had been done, yet the feeling was most intense. Is this all "nerves," or may it not be due to dimly-recalled memories of other lives lived in one or other of these countries?

In all essential ways these curious phases of consciousness which we have just reviewed, agree exactly in character with the memory-summaries of this life. Applying to them the same tests that we would apply to the memories of our present incarnation, are we not justified in regarding them as memories of past lives? In doing so no new principle of memory is involved, it should be noted, for memory works in precisely the same manner whether it extends over years or lives.

The detailed memory of past lives. It must be granted, however, that if reincarnation is to be justified as a process of moral education, the detailed memories of the past must reside somewhere in our consciousness. Otherwise, how would it be possible for us to know that a certain portion of our present destiny was causally related to a certain act or acts in a past life? Do detailed memories of the past exist, and if so, where do they reside?— *that* is the question.

Of recent years some very significant discoveries have been made by psychologists regarding the recovery of forgotten memories. It was found that when a person was thrown into what is known as the hypnotic trance, or even into the half-asleep condition, the memories of the past years of this life could be recovered in detail. In one case a young lady was able to tell where she was, how she was dressed, what she ate, what she said and to whom, on a certain afternoon twelve years prior to the experiment. While awake she had not the slightest recollection of the events of that afternoon, but in the hypnotic trance she apparently remembered them as easily as if they had happened yesterday.

This experiment and many others show beyond question that in the consciousness of every one of us reside literally millions of detailed memories of this life, of which the *waking* consciousness knows nothing. This fact shows how feeble is the trite argument that if in our waking consciousness we do not remember the details of our past lives, it is proof that we have not lived before. This argument is a two-edged sword, for it can be used to "prove" that we have not lived through many of the events of our present incarnation, because we cannot remember them in our waking consciousness.

If the memories of the earlier years of this life can be brought forward in detail into the waking consciousness, is there any possibility that in the same way buried memories of other incarnations might be resurrected from some still deeper layer of consciousness? Colonel de Rochas, a *savant* of Paris, is of the opinion that this is possible, for, by a series of hypnotic experiments carried out many years ago, he apparently forced the consciousness of a woman back over four preceding incarnations, each one separated from the last by a period in the unseen world. He did not dare carry the experiments any farther, since the strain upon the subject was evidently too great. These experiments do not prove the truth of reincarnation, but they are profoundly significant and indicate a possible way of obtaining conclusive evidence.

Sometimes memories of past lives arise spontaneously in the waking consciousness of people. Nearly always, however, these memories are so fragmentary that they are rarely of any value as evidence. Of what use is a bit of scenery, the picture of one's home in a previous life, or the realization of how one was killed, when the name one bore and the country and city in which one lived cannot be recovered? Furthermore, when we take into account the long period which usually intervenes between one incarnation and the next, we see how extraordinarily difficult it is to prove through such fragmentary memories that we really lived at the time recalled.

Young children remember parts of their past incarnations much more frequently than adults, probably because the child-brain is so much more plastic to impressions. Many cases of such child-memories are on record, while not infrequently one meets children who have remembered. Unfortunately, the majority of parents have not the slightest knowledge of reincarnation, and when their children try to tell them of what seems so real to them, they are usually scolded or punished into silence. How much we might learn if only we paid more attention to childish "fancies"! When a child reaches the age of six or seven years whatever memories it may have had generally fade away, probably because the brain is becoming so fully occupied with external impressions.

Sometimes, instead of following the usual plan of remaining a long time in the heaven-world between one incarnation and the next, a man immediately incarnates. In this case the same emotional and mental bodies are used that were organized and trained during the preceding incarnation, and under such circumstances the possibility of remembering many details of the last life is much greater. The strain, however, of two or more physical lives following one another without an intervening period of rest is considerable, and *very* few out of the thousands who die every day are able to stand it. Since the beginning of the war, however, it has been noticed by several investigators that an unusually large number of those soldiers who willingly sacrificed their physical bodies for their country are being reborn immediately. This opportunity, apparently, was earned by them because of their sacrifice, and we may expect them to take an important part in the days of reconstruction, which are to follow, just as soon as their new physical bodies are old enough.

Why we do not remember details of the past.

The physiological reason why, in our waking consciousness, we do not remember the details of our past incarnations is that neither the brain, nor the emotional body, nor the mental body, which we are using this incarnation, were in existence during that past. They have experienced the events of this incarnation only, and therefore the memories impressed upon them are of this incarnation and no other. It is true that occasionally fragments of scenes of past lives are caught by them, but this is quite abnormal.

The detailed memories of the past are within reach only of the soul-consciousness, and not until we have evolved to that exceedingly lofty level where we can unite our waking consciousness with that of the ego will it be possible for us to recall at all completely the details of the past. The soul-consciousness at all times does remember, however, and because of this the very source and center of our consciousness, the evolving ego, is able to understand the meaning of many a lesson which we, in our waking consciousness, cannot grasp at all. In other words, to that superconsciousness of ours, the soul or ego, there is not the slightest injustice in any part of our destinies. It is only our waking consciousness, limited as it is to the knowledge and memories of one physical life, that imagines there is injustice and chance in the world.

The necessity of forgetfulness. The fact that forgetfulness of the past is universal ought to suggest to us that it is best for us not to remember the

details of other incarnations. A little consideration shows quite plainly that such memories, instead of being helpful, would be an actual handicap, if not a curse.

It is certain, for example, that in the past we
have made many moral blunders, because in no
other way could we have developed moral strength.
We may have seen our mistake since then and grown
so strong that our incarnations now are clean and
wholesome; but nevertheless if all the events of the
past formed part of our memory, we should have
each new incarnation to carry around with us an
exceedingly unpleasant set of mental pictures.
Think what would happen if memories of this sort
kept surging up into the mind of a child, especially
during the period of adolescence. They would surely exert a most unwholesome influence and probably ruin the whole incarnation. There is no better
way to insure the purity of a physical incarnation
than to blot out all details of past mistakes, leaving
only the summaries of the lessons learned from
those mistakes in the form of a warning conscience.

Or again, suppose that in the past we grew to
hate, for some foolish reason, a very worthy person. Blinded by unreasoning prejudice we refused
to see anything good in that person. What a serious
handicap it would be if, at the beginning of every
incarnation, the old recollections of those past
hatreds formed part of our consciousness. Whenever we met that person again, whether in a new
physical body or not, it would probably be quite

impossible for us to override the old prejudice. As it is, with the slate of memory wiped clean and the old prejudices forgotten, we meet the one we hated in a new incarnation and find in him much to admire and love. Forgetfulness of the past makes possible, therefore, a much better understanding of our fellows.

In a hundred other ways it can be seen that forgetfulness is imperative. To start anew each life, even so far as memory alone is concerned, prevents lopsided development, the repetition of mistakes by force of previous example, the continuance of racial and religious prejudices, the revival of bad habits such as worry of faultfinding, the useless feeling of remorse for long-past mistakes. Because we cannot remember the details of the past we have no means of anticipating the possible future, which in itself is a great boon, for if we had the power to see what was coming in the future by the study of past causes, we should add to every trial all the pains of anticipation.

The investigation of past lives. When one has reached what is called Initiation, and has undergone the long and arduous training in physical, moral, and mental development which that implies, there is the possibility, by awakening a certain set of psychic faculties, of investigating directly every detail of a whole series of past lives either of oneself or of another. There exists in the mental world what may be called the great memory of Nature, in which every physical event, every desire, every least thought of man and every other living thing is registered with photographic exactness. From these records of the past complete information about any series of incarnations may be obtained by the properly-trained investigator in the form of living pictures. There are several other ways also by which this same information may be gained, but perhaps the best method is this one of letting the living pictures of the past roll before the trained vision. There are a few experts who can do this, and to them reincarnation is no longer a logical and convincing theory; it is a fact.

CHAPTER 7

THE HOPE OF THE WORLD

The menacing growth of materialism and the consequent dimming of the realization of a Divine Presence within the universe has brought civilization to a dangerous crisis in its history. Whenever in the past the pure flame of spiritual understanding flickered and began to pale, the moral nature of the people weakened, and, though the intellect still was keen and subtle, the civilization of the time rapidly fell into decay.

We are now faced by a similar state of things. The trained intellect of man has wrought wonders in the domain of science and invention; but the neglected moral nature has been powerless to guide such activity along wholesome and brotherly lines. There has hardly been a scientific discovery which has not been misused. We invent explosives, not to wrest precious metals from the crust of the earth, but to maim and kill our fellow-men. We learn the principles of aviation and journey through the air, not for the benefit of civilization, but to destroy children and to blast fair cities.

What teaching can most quickly bring man to the

full realization that God *does* exist, and that there *is* a moral law, because whatever seeds of good and evil a man sows in the field of life, the harvests grown must be reaped by him alone? Reincarnation is that teaching and it is, therefore, the hope of the world. It makes possible the belief in the existence of God, even to the scientific mind, for it welds together in a marvelous fashion the facts discovered by science with the half-understood truths of religion. It is the hope of the world because it gives back to us absolute trust in the goodness of the Divine by showing that there is a moral purpose in evolution as well as a physical end.

In the ultramaterialistic days of the last century, when every new discovery seemed to make more terrible the damning conclusion that there could be no God because Nature was cruel, merciless, "red in tooth and claw," it is little wonder that men fell away from the teachings of religion by hundreds of thousands. Even today, when the tide is turning against materialism, the number of the churchless is greater than the churched. The vision of physical evolution *alone* reveals a wonderful plan for the shaping of physical bodies, but it leads either to agnosticism or to atheism.

When, in addition to this, we force ourselves to look closely into the lives and affairs of men, so as to see without glamor just what is taking place in the world, we shrink back appalled by the suffering, the misery, the degradation, the ignorance, the selfishness, and the cruelty found everywhere.

Can this be God-caused? we ask ourselves; can the Deity we worship be responsible either directly or indirectly for all this hideous fantasy? If we blind our eyes with dogmas, and stuff our ears with platitudes, it is possible to get along quite comfortably with never a religious qualm or doubt, but if we look at mankind with unveiled vision, as few dare to do, we are lost on an ocean of doubt.

This is the unhappy position of many people today. They are adrift, with all the old anchors gone. They know not what to do nor from what quarter to look for help. They go hopefully to their spiritual advisors and receive only those teachings from which seemingly all feeling of reality has been drained. They attend divine worship and come away more dissatisfied than before. They visit various sects and schools and movements, and become only confused.

Of one thing, above all else, they demand definite assurance: Is there a Divine purpose back of all the show of the world? They realize that the tiny intellect of man may not be able to understand the nature of a cosmic God, if one exists, but they do ask for some understanding of the purpose of life. If God does exist, what is He trying to do in the world? To what end is mankind struggling?

For it is a struggle! To one who has walked with pitying eyes through the fetid slums of a great metropolis there seems to be little evidence of any Divine purpose. It is all so hopelessly wretched and ugly and depressing. To one who mingles with

the wealthy and the great, how often such existence seems only a training school in the refinements
of selfishness. Thoughtless disregard of the wel-
fare of others, luxury and glitter cloaking moral
laxity, intellects busied with pleasing trifles, show
us all too plainly the tragedy of wealth. Quarrels
and hatreds, crimes and jealousies, passions and
prejudices, are hard to reconcile with the loving
care of God. Oh, it is easy to see why early religious thinkers fell back upon the theory of a Satan
tempting man to wrong, and the Fall of the first
pair when they ate of the fruit of knowledge of good
and evil.

We can no longer accept these ancient specula-
tions to explain the evils of the world, for we are
no longer convinced of the historicity of the legends
upon which they are based, but, unfortunately for
our peace of mind, we have found no logical explanation to take their place.

We stand at the cross-roads. Behind us is the
long and weary road we have traversed, which began
upon the distant hill-top of simple faith, wound
through the vale of daily life, crossed the bridge of
doubt, and descended into the valley of disbelief.
Insensibly we have commenced to mount again,
and before us as pilgrims, stretch two roads. One
leads to scientific agnosticism, where spiritual
things are ignored and forgotten; the other leads to
such a splendid interpretation of the purpose of life
that we regain all our old sense of the nearness of
God and all our old trust in His goodness and love.

The clue leading us along this road is Reincarnation.

In the opinion of many, Christianity can regain its hold upon the minds and hearts of thoughtful people who have left the Churches only by commencing to teach again its long-forgotten truth of reincarnation. Ever since about the middle of the sixth century the Christian teaching of the pre-existence and reincarnation of the soul has been lost sight of, primarily because of the intellectual and moral darkness which swept over Europe with the coming of the barbarians from the north. Those barbarians have now become civilized and constitute the leading nations of the world. It is high time that the lost truth of reincarnation be placed again among the priceless treasures of Christendom.

If this is not done the number of the churchless will continually become greater, for the existing dogmas of the Church do not interpret life and the purpose of life in a manner satisfactory to the highly-trained modern intellect. But if reincarnation is once more restored to the place of honor, then the Church can explain life logically and wholesomely, and at the same time drive home many a moral lesson by showing us the Divine Purpose and the splendid goal of evolution made possible by reincarnation.

Reincarnation gives perspective, a true sense of values, the feeling of Eternity. It awakens wonder, stirs our imagination, and sends our gaze wandering down the vistas of the centuries. It is inspiration to poet, light to philosopher, joy to saint, for it tells of the way to God.

How stirring is the romance of the past! We have hunted in the forests as savages; as peasants we have toiled in the fields; the armies of long-forgotten kings and Pharaohs numbered us in their ranks; we have reveled in the debauchery of voluptuous cities of buried civilizations; as merchants we have trafficked in fabrics made on looms that had crumbled into dust before known history began. We have worshiped God under many names, and each time the form of religion into which we were born seemed the only one for man. We bowed before the dark images in the mighty temples of ocean-covered Atlantis; with hearts of joy we laid flowers at the feet of the gods of Egypt; we fell in reverence when the divine Fire flashed down upon a Zoroastrian altar; we made offerings before Vishnu in the rock-hewn temples of Ind; we wore the yellow robe of Buddha and chanted the rules of the Noble Eight-fold Path; we poured out joyous libations before the fair gods in the marble fanes of Greece; we followed rigidly the stern decrees of the Roman law, and perchance were of those who gathered around the unknown Teacher as He walked and taught in Palestine, and our narrow views outraged by what He said and did, threw stones at Him, a blasphemous vagabond! We lived in the Middle Ages the austere life of priest or nun; and now—we have returned to earth to worship again the Eternal God and tread once more the round of birth and life and death in this wonderful old World-School.

QUEST BOOKS

Other Quest books about reincarnation

CATHARS AND REINCARNATION
By Arthur Guirdham
An English girl remembers her 13th century life as a heretic.

EXPERIENCING REINCARNATION
By James S. Perkins
A first person account of the technique of reincarnation.

REINCARNATION
By Leoline L. Wright
What reincarnates and why don't we remember?

REINCARNATION: EAST WEST ANTHOLOGY
Comp. by Joseph Head and S. L. Cranston
Comments from over 400 world famous people on this concept.

REINCARNATION: FACT OR FALLACY?
By Geoffrey Hodson
An inquiry into the evidence for the rebirth theory.

REINCARNATION IN CHRISTIANITY
By Geddes MacGregor
Is the rebirth concept compatible with Christian dogma?

THROUGH DEATH TO REBIRTH
By James S. Perkins
A study of the nature and method of reincarnation.

WHEEL OF REBIRTH
By H. K. Challoner
An autobiographical account of the author's past lives.

These titles are available from:
QUEST BOOKS
306 West Geneva Road
Wheaton, Illinois 60187